Semi-Retirement

Based on a True Story

Finding, Buying, and Running a Bed and Breakfast Inn

Alder Blackburn

Semi-retirement

This is a work of fiction. Names, characters, places, and incidents are the product of the author's imagination or are used fictitiously. Any resemblance to actual persons, living or dead, events, or locales is entirely coincidental.

All rights reserved
Copyright © 2012 by Alder Blackburn

Interior Book Design and Layout by
www.integrativeink.com

ISBN: 978-0-615-57791-3

No part of this publication may be reproduced, stored in a retrieval system, or transmitted in any form or by any means electronic, mechanical, photocopying, recording, or otherwise, without the written permission of the author or publisher.

Table of Contents

CHAPTER 1
    THE DECISION 1

CHAPTER 2
    SEARCH DAY 1 17

CHAPTER 3
    SEARCH DAY 2 37

CHAPTER 4
    SEARCH DAY 3 55

CHAPTER 5
    FINDING PRIMROSE INN 77

CHAPTER 6
    SELL A HOUSE, BUY AN INN 93

CHAPTER 7
    MOVING IN 131

CHAPTER 8
    EARLY DAYS 146

CHAPTER 9
    BEING AN INNKEEPER 169

CHAPTER 10
    STAFF AND GUEST STORIES 193

CHAPTER 11
    IS THIS WORTH IT? 215

CHAPTER 12
   THANKSGIVING 221
Addendum 253

CHAPTER 1

The Decision

"I thought that you were never going to suggest it!" she said.

"But I've only just thought up the idea," I replied. "A little hint or two on the direction you were thinking, or that you wanted me to be thinking, might have been helpful."

Doris—sometimes known as Dolly, my wife of more than forty years—and I had retired some two years earlier when we were both in our mid-sixties. We now resided on a sea island off the coast of South Carolina, and after two years, we were beginning to feel the pinch—both mentally and financially. It was not simply that the cost of living there was high; it was also that there were more and more assessments for more and more money to be spent on more and more projects handed down from the management to "improve" the fancy golf club, of which we were once happy but now steadily sinking into becoming reluctant members.

We were now on a fixed income, and for the first time in our lives, we had to learn to be more fiscally responsible. We were not doing a very good job. Up to this point in our lives, there had always been an adequate income, and thinking more than twice about spending on other than major projects was rarely necessary. For the most part, I was the one who needed to go through the learning curve. Doris had always been better about keeping her feet on the ground and staying responsible. I was also the more dramatic; Doris was calmer and more thoughtful.

Through the large picture window in the back of the house, I could see out onto the seventeenth green of one of the two courses provided by the fancy golf club. It was this green that was on my mind now.

"We've got to do something!" I said. "Pretty soon, there will be no more nest egg, no more life of Riley, no more obligatory nights eating in the restaurant at the club, and hello food line. Plus, when everything is taken into consideration, life around here is pretty routine and boring, don't you agree?"

Doris and I had known each other since our early teens, growing up in the same town in England. We married in our early twenties, and within a year of getting married, we immigrated to the United States. We had three children, all boys, and now all of them married. There were four grandchildren—three boys and one precious little baby girl to break the pattern. We had been blessed with reasonably good health and had thus far enjoyed a good life.

Earlier in our lives, we'd settled in a suburb of Columbus, Ohio, where we finished raising our family—after which Doris returned to the work force. I was lucky to enjoy a rewarding career in the pharmaceutical industry; however, during the 1980s and 1990s, the larger pharmaceutical companies either purchased outright or at least purchased the assets of the smaller companies, then merged and moved them. I was too old to adapt to the ways of new big pharma, so I took the earliest opportunity presented to retire.

Doris went back to work when the boys were old enough to be left. She first worked for the CEO of a large local corporation, and later for one of the more flamboyant board members, Jim French. Doris would travel with Jim in his private jet to different locations where Jim had an interest. She looked after his family and saw that his houses were staffed and maintained. There was also a significant social obligation on her to entertain business associates in Columbus.

I was traveling a considerable amount for my job at that time also. Our boys were grown by this time and more than able to take care of themselves. Returning to Columbus after business trips for one or both of us was a time to relax and just enjoy being a family. We weren't rich, but we were certainly well off.

Vacations were fun. We love the beach and warm weather, so when we were in a position to buy a beach house on a sea island off the South Carolina coast, we took the opportunity. Buying the beach house meant that we had to join the club, but that was okay. It provided us with the opportunity to play golf and tennis, which the boys adored; we could also use the swimming pools and restaurant in the clubhouse. In truth, we had to spend $200 a month for food in the club as a part of their rules. That was never a problem for us with boys and their friends, and later their wives. Life was good.

Two years ago, when I was sixty-five and Doris was sixty-four, the idea of retirement began to appeal to us. We would simply sell our house in Ohio, sell our vacation house in South Carolina, and buy a bigger house on our island down south. The vacations that we had enjoyed in the past would become our permanent way of life. What more could one ask for? So without much more thought, we did it. We planned to walk the beach every day, play golf when we wanted, and laze away our time with good books, comfortably sitting in the sun.

Of course, that is not the way things turned out. Without the children, Doris and I were left to walk the beach alone, and my golf score never did get to much less than 100, no matter how hard I tried. Life became very much a routine without a challenge; the routine became the challenge. On top of this, we were going through money faster than anticipated.

The biggest problem, the one that confronted us most, came in the form of assessments handed down by the club. The managing committee wanted to upgrade the facilities to attract a newer and younger membership, and their choice of payment for these upgrades was to charge the existing members by way of assessments—extra payments each month on your club bill. They assured everybody that by upgrading, they were increasing the value of our investment. Since most of the other members had unlimited sources of income, or so it seemed, the assessments usually passed the voting procedure.

Their latest assessment to raise money came to us through the mail.

"Listen to this," Doris had said, waving the letter in her hand to get my attention. "They want to charge us a fee to kill all the grass on the greens, and then reseed them with grass that's more tolerant to salt water."

I shook my head. I wasn't surprised. I'd heard the rumors.

"Why?" she asked.

"Well, this way they can water the greens more frequently," I told her. "Most of the well water here has a lot of salt in it, and the salt makes the grass turn brown—even kills it. This new grass handles the salt differently, better actually, so the greens can be watered more frequently and will have fewer brown patches. Besides," I added, "they've just done the very same thing on Kiawah, and we don't want their greens to be greener greens than our greens, do we?"

"I don't care," was Doris's response. "And I really don't understand."

"But you *do* understand that it will cost us more money each month on our club bill."

"*That,* I understand. I'm not an idiot," Doris said. "The question is: what are you going to do about it?"

SEMI-RETIREMENT

This now meant that the ball had been well and truly thrown into my court, and it was up to me to find a solution to how to pay for a higher club bill. There followed several days, maybe weeks, of what-to-do ideas before I made the latest suggestion, which apparently was the one Doris had been waiting for me to make.

"I think that we should sell this house and buy a bed and breakfast. It will give us something to do and will also provide an additional income," I said. "As long as we can find a place that is large enough to support a staff so that we don't have to do any of the heavy lifting or cleaning, just manage the place, it should all work out perfectly for us. Be sort of like semi-retirement instead of this real retirement unreal situation that we are in right now."

"I thought that you were never going to come up with that suggestion," Doris said, exasperated.

After this exchange and a very poignant silence, Doris said, "How are you going to go about it?"

"Well," and I had to think quickly here, "you remember the B&B where we stayed a few times in Ashville? I can't remember its name, but it's run by that guy Frank Thornton."

"Beechview House," Doris said, nodding.

She was way ahead of me, as usual, and her memory had always been better than mine. "Yes," I said, "Beechview House. Old Frank is such an amiable man. We'll ask his advice. And didn't he say that his inn was for sale?"

"I don't want to buy that inn." Doris was making a point and establishing ground rules about what was to be our search for a new way of life. "Frank's inn has been looking pretty run down lately."

"But you will agree to drive up there and talk to Frank, won't you?"

"Oh yes. It will do us good to get a night away, and we often have our best discussions when we're in the car and you have to listen."

"I'll get him on the phone then and make a reservation."

I was getting into a groove about what we were exploring, and I had a vague memory of Frank mentioning that his inn was going up for sale. Frank's inn was just about perfect for what I had in mind; all I had to do was sell the idea to Doris.

Frank answered his phone, "Beechview House."

"Frank, this is Derick Anderson," I said. "We've stayed with you a few times in the past."

"Who is it?"

"Derick Anderson," I repeated, a bit louder. "My wife Doris and I have stayed with you a few times."

There was silence on the other end, and then, "Oh, the limeys," said Frank. "Yes, I remember you."

"Well, we would like to come up and stay tomorrow night if you have an opening, and I want to sit down with you, pick your brain, and ask your advice about something that I have on my mind."

"Tomorrow you say? Yes, that will be okay. We only have a woman and her daughter booked in tomorrow. Do you want the same room that you had the last time? And what time do you plan to arrive?"

"Same room is fine, and we should get there around 5:00 PM." Then I asked, "When would be a good time to pick your brain?"

"After breakfast the next day," he replied. "Betty and I have a dinner date tomorrow evening."

"Okay, that's great then. See you tomorrow." I hung up the phone.

Doris nodded in confirmation, then gently reminded me, "We're just going to ask Frank some questions, right? I don't want to buy that inn."

"Yes, Dolly, my love," I said. "Ask questions. We won't buy Frank's inn."

Some days it was hard to stay ahead of Doris.

The journey up Interstate 26 was uneventful. We've always enjoyed driving from the Low Country through the Midlands and into the Up Country in South Carolina. Beechview House was just over the state line between South Carolina and North Carolina

Pulling in and getting our first glimpse of the inn, it seemed just fine to me. I couldn't imagine what Doris's problem with it was. The house wasn't old, but it had been built to look old. There were five bedrooms, plus an owner's suite. The owner's suite used to be the servants' quarters before the house was converted to a bed and breakfast.

The house was set on five acres, bordering a golf course, and the acreage was simply landscaped for easy upkeep. There were open spaces for outdoor functions and a small parking lot that could only handle enough cars for overnight guests. The lot next door was empty, and I knew that Frank ignored many local ordnances and rules and often used space in this open lot for overflow parking.

Frank Thornton and his wife Betty had been running the inn for about ten years, well past the average burnout time for innkeepers, which tended to be seven and a half years. Frank would be in his mid-seventies by now, but he didn't look it and still appeared to be quite active. Betty was younger, and she still had a job outside the inn, something to do with administration on the Biltmore estate. Doris had inferred in the past that Betty only kept her job because it provided her with time away from Frank, who, according to Doris, could be a bit of an old bore. I'd never given that much thought. I kind of liked the guy.

The Thornton's were anglophiles, top to bottom and through and through. They had decorated their house with many pieces of old but somewhat questionable antique furniture from England, and their walls were covered with prints of fox hunting scenes and village green cricket. Maybe this is why I liked the place. Maybe I couldn't see past all this folderol to the frayed edges underneath. And as I've said, I sort of liked old Frank Thornton. I've never found him in a bad mood and always enjoyed his company. Not a bit of a bore to me. Living the good life, I was sure.

Both Thorntons were out when we arrived. There was an envelope on a desk just inside the door with our names on it and a note inside that read, *"Your room is ready. We're out for the evening. See you at breakfast tomorrow. Can't wait for our chat."*

Doris wanted to know why he couldn't wait for a chat when he knew nothing about why we were there.

We carried our bags into the room where we had stayed in the past. Doris pointed out a new burn mark on the carpet in the shape of an iron.

"Looks like somebody wanted to take some creases out and didn't give a hoot about the carpet," she said. "Who irons on the floor anyway? Some people! Frank needs to upgrade this place, you know. It's getting a tatty look to it."

I opened the bag with our traveling bar and fixed a couple of drinks. Frank had left glasses and a small bucket of ice. Good memory or good note keeping, I thought to myself.

"How about dinner, Doris?" I asked, after we had our first cocktail. "What do you fancy?"

"Nothing over the top considering our circumstances," she said, "and I would hate to run into Frank and Betty, who no doubt are wining and dining in the fanciest restaurant in town."

"Come on, Dolly, what about Angelfish?"

"I thought you'd never ask."

SEMI-RETIREMENT

* * *

Next morning, the mother and daughter guests were already seated at a large table in the dining room when we arrived for breakfast. The set up at Beechview House was for everybody to sit around one large table and not at small separate ones. Another point of contention for Doris. Doris has noted often that she prefers small, individual tables, so if you don't feel like talking to the other guests, you don't feel obliged to.

"Good morning." We nodded at each other and smiled. "Wonder what we have on offer this morning?"

The mother and daughter just kept on smiling and nodding, nothing more was said. I just hate being in those situations when you don't know whether you should shut up or try and force the conversation. I had to think to myself that Doris was right about small, individual tables, but then our host entered with a steaming pot of coffee.

"Good morning, everybody." Frank was in top form. "Everybody slept well, I'm sure. Derick, Doris good to see you again. Coffee?"

The coffee was served, and then Alma appeared with the entrée. Alma was an African American woman who worked for Frank and Betty. She had been there every morning when we had stayed in the past. She wasn't young but seemed to be spry. There was always a smile and a cheery hello. We always left her a decent tip in our room after each stay because we knew that she had the additional responsibility of housekeeping chores. Maybe her smile was a *thank you* for past favors.

"Sausage, fried eggs, and toast this morning. Sausage comes from Piggly Wiggly; nothing but the best," Alma announced.

The daughter across the table spoke up.

"I'm a vegan," she said. "I'm afraid that I can't eat a breakfast like that."

"Well, you should have let us know before now," Frank said, "because all that we have for you then is toast. Will you be all right with just toast? You're not gluten free as well, I hope."

I could tell that she was disappointed, and of course Frank had been out the night before so wasn't around to find out about any dietary restrictions, but she smiled and nodded again. "Just toast will do nicely," she replied.

There was more aggressiveness in his demeanor than I remembered in the past. He talked about the weather. He asked about our favorite sporting teams and wanted to know what plans we had for the rest of the day.

"Well, not the Andersons," he said. "I know what you want, and that is to chat with me."

The mother and daughter clearly didn't want to engage in a long conversation. They said that they were touring and would probably visit the Biltmore, and that they would be leaving directly after breakfast.

"I'll prepare your bill then," said Frank, and off he went to his office. We were all left with another round of smiles and nods but no further conversation.

"I've got your ticket ready, too, Derick," Frank said, when he came back into the room. "I still don't know what you want to ask, but I thought that I'd get your money first in case you don't like what I tell you."

Both parties handed over credit cards, and he processed them.

The mother and daughter were soon saying goodbye and walking out with their suitcases. Alma was clearing the table and getting ready for her housekeeping chores while Frank, Doris, and I sat down in wingback chairs in the living room, each of us with a fresh cup of steaming coffee. They made excellent coffee in that inn.

SEMI-RETIREMENT

I needed to establish myself again, as Frank was still being unusually intimidating. I tried lowering my voice and projecting my words, enunciating with authority. This is never an easy thing to do when Doris is around because she instinctively knows what I'm up to. She has it all figured out and will one day give a superb impersonation of me trying to control this very conversation. But it had to be done.

"Frank...." And then I cleared my throat. "We need to know all that there is to know about the bed and breakfast business."

"Nobody can answer that," Frank replied with a guffaw. "The bed and breakfast business is incredibly complex, and every innkeeper has his own interpretation of how to run his own inn." Frank was old school, and his answers were all in the masculine. Maybe that was one of the things that gave Doris problems.

"Well, what about you? What is your interpretation then?" I pressed.

"Me, I just let the place run itself. I do very little around here. I can't be bothered with the books. Betty takes care of all of that. In truth, she sends the paperwork out and some bookkeeper somewhere crunches the numbers. Betty also arranges and prepares the breakfasts. Sometimes Alma and I help with the final preparation. Alma takes care of the housekeeping with help from her friends when we're very busy. I'm just the straw boss around here. My job is to see that things get done. Oh, I suppose that I'm a concierge of sorts as well. Tell folks where to find good food and what to see and do around the area."

So much for the masculine, I thought, but then I asked, "That's it? You don't do anything except help where needed and everything gets delegated?"

"Right on," said Frank, smiling. "Pretty good gig, this inn keeping business. You make okay money, pay very few taxes, and find others to do the heavy lifting."

"Then why are you selling?" I wanted to know.

"Selling! Ha, you mean sold," Frank replied. "Shook hands on the transfer last night."

"Congratulations, Frank," I said, but I was a little taken aback. "The last two times we stayed here, you mentioned that the inn was for sale. It must have been on the market for over a year."

"Just had it listed in all the wrong places. All those *experts*, the ones who write the books and run the bed and breakfast consulting companies, have about as much idea of what they're talking about as I would if I tried to explain flying to the moon. One ad, taken out by yours truly, Frank Thornton, in the *Wall Street Journal* was all that it took, and I had a buyer in two days. He's moving here from Florida next month."

"Well, good for you, Frank. I guess that it's too late for me to make an offer now."

"Is that what this is all about? Are you thinking of buying this inn?"

"Well, not exactly *this* inn, Frank," I said, glancing at Doris. "We wanted to get an idea from you of what it takes to run an inn before we make a decision to buy one."

"Straw boss and concierge," Frank said again. "There really are no rules. Just use your intuition. Whatever you do, don't listen to those bloody experts; their heads are way too high up in their behinds. I admire them for taking your money, but you don't need their aspiring innkeeper courses or their how-to books—it's all just good common sense. Straw boss and concierge." Frank leaned forward a little in his chair. "Look, you are unique; your inn will be unique. There won't be another like it anywhere in the world. If you're talking about managing a single branch of a chain motel, then maybe somebody should write down some rules so that your branch is the same as the branch in the next town. But in this situation, in a bed and breakfast that you own, you make the rules and they will be your own rules specific to your operation. You don't need to know more than how to be a Straw boss and concierge."

"Frank, there has to be more to it," I said, still not believing it could be that simple.

"There's not," he said, sitting back. "Straw boss and concierge. Go to the Internet. It's easy to find what's out there for sale. Better yet, buy a copy of the *Wall Street Journal*, pick out an inn that interests you, and go for it."

I had thought that I needed to know a lot more. Things like business plans, associations, advertising, promotion, financing, occupancy rates, and how to price the rooms. Not to mention management, housekeeping, and a million other things. Obviously Frank was neither in the mood nor inclined to offer any more advice than he already had. Maybe he was right; maybe it was all an intuitive thing and everything is very individualistic.

I was somewhat taken aback and feeling foolish that we had driven all this way to get advice that could easily have been given over the telephone. I was also feeling a little let down and certainly stumped on what to ask him next.

"What will you do now, Frank?"

"I'm not sure," he said. "And I'm maybe a little worried. I need something to do. But then you might have given me an idea. Maybe I'll offer a course on running a bed and breakfast or write a how-to book. If a bright spark like you is asking questions, just think of all the money I can make off the other duller knives in the drawer."

"Don't listen to him, Derick." Doris had had enough of the conversation. "He's blowing smoke at you now."

"Smart woman, that wife of yours, Derick." Frank went on. "The two of you would be a perfect team running a B&B—legends you'll become in no time."

"Thanks, Frank," I replied, getting up. "It's been real."

"Real," Doris added.

Frank got to his feet. Big smile across his face, eyes twinkling away, hand stretched out as always to shake goodbye.

"Good luck to you," he said. "Stay in touch."

"Goodbye Frank, and say our goodbyes to Betty and Alma." Doris added another "Real" as we left.

Frank was off into his new world. Having just sold his inn, I got the impression that he preferred not to be talking about his old way of life but rather making plans for his future. We were an unwanted distraction.

Back in the car heading south, the journey back home was anything but dull.

"Did you believe him?" I asked Doris.

"More important, did *you* believe him?" Doris asked me. "You're the one who had the cockamamie idea."

"But you're the one who couldn't wait for me to make the suggestion," I reminded her.

"Huh," was all she uttered about that.

"Remember, we *do* have a problem," I added. "We've got to do something about our finances. Our current situation is untenable; the greenest greens on the golf course are turning our bank balance red."

Backwards and forwards we went with the conversation. At one time, one of us would take the pro position about buying an inn, and the other was con. Then we reversed, and then reversed again. Doris was not as impressed with Frank Thornton's arguments as I had been, but she did somewhat see his point. More importantly, we both knew that something had to be done about our circumstances, and changes had to be made to our current way of life. It turned out that neither of us was intimidated by the thought of inn keeping, which was a good thing.

At no point during the journey did we both fall on the con side, but it took the whole drive from Ashville to the outskirts of Charleston before we both fell into the pro camp.

"However," Doris said, "there has to be criteria. I'm not going to agree to buy any old inn just because we are going to buy an inn. Or a bed and breakfast, or whatever you want to call it."

"Of course," I agreed, trying desperately to think what her criteria might be so that I could say it first and impress her.

"What about an inn with a restaurant?" I asked.

"Absolutely not," was the response.

"Of course," I said, shaking my head. "That is the *last* thing that we want." I hoped that Doris couldn't see through my attempt at keeping her enthusiastic about the overall project.

"What else?" I asked.

"No mountain tops or deep forests," Doris said. "We need to be in or near enough to a city so that we can go on enjoying all the conveniences that we are used to."

I readily agreed. "Of course."

"Something with some class—not just another old house."

"Gotcha."

"Stay in the South—nowhere where we have to shovel snow."

"Right on," I agreed. "Dolly, you're getting into the groove with this now."

"Not too big," she went on. "We need something that we can manage."

"Probably can't afford anything too big," I said.

"You'd better be listening to me, Derick Anderson. I'm being serious, and you are being just a little bit patronizing! This is a big change for us, and even if it's maybe something that you have always had a hankering to do, that is *not* the case with me. I'm doing this for you, remember?"

"That's not it, Dolly," I protested. "We basically have no choice."

Silence.

By fortune, we were now approaching our garage door. "I'll check the listings on the Internet and come up with places for us to check out based on the criteria," I said. "But first, I'm going to fix a drink."

"Fix one for me, too," she said cheerily, as she hopped out of the car and into the house. "It's been an interesting couple of days."

CHAPTER 2

Search Day 1

There are a wealth of places on the Internet where one can go to retrieve listings of Bed and Breakfast Inns for sale. Most list geographically, which helped, as I was putting our list together and trying to follow Doris's criteria.

No restaurant, no way out in the country location, south of the Mason Dixon line, interesting looking facility, not too big. I realized that we were going to have to make some compromises. I also realized that it was far too early in this project for me to share any kind of compromise with Doris. It seemed to me that she would need to be shown what was available, and the compromise would be based on how well she liked a particular property.

I decided on two lists, to keep the criteria list as a very low profile. One list would be inns that met *most* of what we were looking for, and the second list would be inns that met only *some* of the criteria. I wasn't trying to fool Doris, or pull the wool over her eyes—she was far too bright to fall for that. I reasoned that by casting a wide net, we stood a better chance of catching more little fish—and maybe a big one would find its way in there as well. Anyway, one list would be inns that met most of the criteria, and so we would need to go inside and look it over. The second list would be inns of interest only, and a drive-by for this first encounter would be sufficient.

Inn number one: "Bluebell Acres," small country location south of Charlotte and not too far from the Interstate. Possibly a drive-by look; only make an appointment if the drive-by interested us.

Inn number two: "The Generals' Quarters," medium size, small town south of Atlanta. Actually not too far from Hartsfield International Airport. Certainly a look inside; quite high on the list.

Inn number three: "Preston Hall," small but with great potential. Way out in the country in West Virginia but with a lot of personal interest, as it had been built by an English Aristocrat so there was a bit of a link there. Anyway, it was somewhere that I wanted to see; good price and more than 30 acres of land. Doris might just fall for it, too. Appointment needed because of its location.

Inn number four: "Harmony Hotel," Leesburg, Virginia. Small hotel but very inexpensive. Drive-by at best.

Inn number five: "The Magnolia House," small town outside Fayetteville, North Carolina. The asking price was quite high, but it filled all of the criteria. Certainly an appointment here.

Inn number six: "Historic Primrose Inn," Versailles, Kentucky. Medium size but maybe a little too far north and nowhere we had visited, so completely unknown. Drive-by, low on the list.

Inn number seven: "Brookfield House," Southern Pines in North Carolina. Small inn but a lot like Frank Thornton's place. On the list because my first choice of Beechview had been sold out from under my feet. Drive-by only.

Inn number eight: "The Old Doctor's House," another small town in Georgia. Good size and good price, but only a drive-by.

Inn number nine: "The Captain's Retreat," New Berne, North Carolina. Maybe too large, with fifteen rooms, but otherwise fitting all other criteria. Certainly an appointment.

SEMI-RETIREMENT

Inn number ten: "Magnolia," single word. Located in Athens, Georgia. Seemed to be ideal, but keep as drive-by.

Inn number eleven: "Mountainside Inn," actually located in Blacksburg, Virginia and not on a mountain. Smallish but well worth a visit; appointment necessary.

As I was working on my list, I heard a crash overhead from the general direction of the roof. I had heard this sound before and thought that it was probably an errant golf ball whose intended destination had been the seventeenth green. I stepped out onto the back deck to survey for damage and to look for the ball. I couldn't find any evidence of damage, but I did come across a lonely golf ball with a big "G" written on it. I picked it up.

"Sorry about that, my friend." The voice was coming from a jovial chap who had wandered into the back yard. There was no fence.

"Your friend?" I asked.

"Yes, ugly looking man sitting out there on the cart. Sometimes he really gets a good shot off with great distance, but other times there's a mean slice at the end so the ball ends up way off the fairway, even out of bounds."

"Tell him to tighten his grip at the point of impact," I replied.

"Oh, I've tried that," he said, then he grinned, realizing that he had admitted to ownership of the errant ball. "I end up cutting the ball to the left."

I smiled back and looked just beyond his partner in the golf cart to see another ball lying neatly on the green just a short putt from the hole.

"That's a good looking shot," I said. "But it would look better if the green were greener, don't you think?"

"Green were greener? What do you mean?" He looked very confused.

"Nothing," I replied. "Here's your ball, 'G.' Have a good one."

"Thanks," he said, still looking puzzled. "Sorry 'bout my friend, again." With raised eyebrows, and his head shaking slightly from left to right, he left the yard and threw his ball onto the green, nearly knocking his partner's well placed approach into a greenside bunker.

Once I had established the list, I put together a plan for visiting each of the places selected, made appointments where I thought we would be most interested, and typed up a little background on each location for Doris.

The plan came together as follows:

	Drive-by	Inn 1	Bluebell Acres
Search Day 1	Drive-by	Inn 7	Brookfield House
	Late afternoon appointment	Inn 5	The Magnolia House

Spend the night in Fayetteville, North Carolina.

	Drive-by	Inn 10	Magnolia
Search Day 2	Early afternoon appointment	Inn 2	The Generals' Quarters
	Drive-by	Inn 8	Old Doctor's House

Spend the night in a suitable roadside hotel before returning home and spending a couple of days in South Carolina.

For the second foray, we would start by driving to New Berne, North Carolina and finding a suitable hotel to spend the night.

Search Day 3	Late afternoon appointment	Inn 4	Harmony Hotel
	Early morning appointment	Inn 9	The Captain's Retreat

Spend the night in a suitable roadside hotel.

Search Day 4	Late afternoon appointment	Inn 3	Preston Hall
	Late morning appointment	Inn 11	Mountainside Inn

Spend the night at Preston Hall.

Search Day 5	Drive-by	Inn 6	Historic Primrose Inn

Drive on to spend the night with our middle son in Columbus.

I typed it all up and presented the plan to Doris.

"I can't understand all this Day 1, Inn 7 nonsense," she said. "Just get on with it, and I'll tell you what is acceptable and what isn't."

"Okay," I said, trying to keep the conversation light and knowing full well that I was attempting to slip a few fast ones past her. I also realized that she had probably taken the whole thing in and knew exactly what I was up to.

"I'll make the calls, check the routes, organize hotels, and we'll be off on our adventure."

"You go, guy."

"If you like we can see the three boys as well," I added. " We'll spend some time in Columbus with Alec, I'm not at all sure that he and his wife are getting along very well these days. We'll also try to go to Cleveland for a day with Peter and the children, and if we have time, we'll stop in Cincinnati to see Geoffrey and the kids there."

"Sounds good," she replied, then added, "By the way there were two Magnolias on your list. Are you sure that you haven't gotten things mixed up?"

"No," I said. "We're in the south—one of our criteria—and they're big on the word Magnolia down here."

I thought that I'd won a point but then realized that this was Doris's way of letting me know that she was very much on top of things. Not even a tiny shred of wool was going to be pulled over her eyes.

It came together remarkably well. There would be more than a day back on our island in between days two and three, which was a bother because it was mid-September and usually we try not to be here for the hurricane season, just in case. We had experienced a couple of tropical storms, and no way did we want to be around for a hurricane. But it was what it was, and I gambled that we would most likely be lucky. Prayer would need to be invoked.

The time came to set off. The car was loaded, the GPS set, the details all typed out and organized into manila folders, and a good supply of pens on hand in order for us to write down any thoughts or comments. And a full tank of gas.

Day one included a drive to Charlotte, on to Southern Pines, and finish up in Fayetteville—a busy day but doable. Two drive-bys and one appointment that had been set for 5:00 PM.

SEMI-RETIREMENT

An uneventful journey to our first drive-by mid-morning, Bluebell Acres. The GPS, we call ours "Flo," had no problem getting us to the inn, but thank goodness that it had a sign outside because it was on a country road lined with ordinary looking houses, and the inn was just another one. Nothing special, just a ranch-style house set on its little piece of land on a country road looking for all it's worth the same as all its neighbors.

"That's it?" I was disappointed.

"I would like to see inside," Doris said.

"Doris, this is just a drive-by. If we like the look of the outside and we haven't seen anything that we like better out of the rest on our list, then we'll call and make an appointment to look inside and see more."

"What is the point of being here if we can't see inside?"

"I've just explained the point."

"I would like to see inside."

I knew that I was beaten. Whatever argument I offered up would be lost, and I ran the risk of putting the whole project in jeopardy. I went to my list, found the telephone number, and called.

A woman answered the phone. "Bluebell Acres, can I help you?"

"Please, my name is Derick Anderson, and I have seen a listing that your inn is for sale."

"Yes," she said.

"Is there any way that we might come around and look at it?" I asked.

"Yes. When would you like to come?"

"Well, we're in town now. How about sometime in the next half an hour." I was anxious not to lose too much time on our first stop, especially at a place that really held no interest for me.

"Oh," she said. "We're not meant to let anybody look at the inn without our real estate agent being present."

Oh God! I thought. *Not only do I have to spend time looking at something that I don't want to look at, but I also have to put up with a real estate agent.*

"I'm sorry," I said. "We're just passing through, and it seemed like such a good opportunity."

"If you don't mind, I'll call our agent and see if she can get out here."

"Would you? We'd be very grateful. My name is Derick Anderson, and my wife is Doris."

"What is your number?" she asked. "I'll call you right back."

I gave her my cell phone number, looked at Doris, and said, "Why don't we drive around and see the town and maybe try and find a sandwich for lunch?"

Doris agreed.

There was no town. We drove back and forth and tried to find a central area, but none existed; it was just ranch-style house next to another ranch-style house on the road, and they all looked basically the same. "Flo," our GPS, wasn't any help either. The nearest food of any kind that she found was fast food joints just off the exits and entrances to the freeway.

"I'm not so hungry that I fancy fast food," I said to Doris.

"No, nor am I," she replied, just as the cell phone rang.

"Can you be here in forty-five minutes?" was the question.

"Yes," I said, a little annoyed that my schedule was being thrown off. "Thank you."

"Forty-five minutes," I said to Doris, and she nodded that she understood.

We drove around some more and still found not even a hint of a town. I think that even Doris was becoming disenchanted with our current situation.

"Maybe this is an area where folks who need work in Charlotte live but they prefer to live in the country. Something like that?" I offered.

"Most unusual," Doris said.

We were driving very slowly, so it was very noticeable when this little red car flashed past us in the other direction.

"Maybe late for lunch," I said.

Doris didn't answer.

When forty of the forty-five minutes had passed, we were close again to the Bluebell Acres. As we drove up, I noticed the same little red car parked on the circular drive that fronted the property.

"Not late for lunch. Must have been in a hurry to meet us," Doris said. "You know, I would hate anybody doing to us what we have just done to these poor folks."

"Doris, looking inside was your last minute idea, what can I say? Let's go and look, and then be on our way."

The front of the house had a wide porch and was decked out with several oversized wooden rocking chairs.

"I bet they got that idea from Cracker Barrel," Doris whispered.

The front door was overly ornate, with carved wood and colored glass. We rang the bell.

"Are you the Andersons?" asked a pleasantly dumpy woman of indeterminate age. "My name is Abby Woolums," she said, "and this is my husband, Ralph."

Ralph, standing behind her, appeared older than Abby, even though it was hard to figure out how old Abby was. Ralph hardly acknowledged us—just a nod in our direction indicating that he knew we were there.

"We run Bluebell Acres," Abby said, "and this is Alexia, our real estate agent."

In contrast to Abby, Alexia was drop dead gorgeous. She had a fabulous figure and dressed to show it off to its best advantage. I was beginning to change my mind about real estate agents and the disruption in our plans.

"If you like," Abby said, "I'll show you around, and then if you have any questions, Alexia and I can help with answers."

"Good," I answered. *I must be sure that I have plenty of questions,* I thought. *But what the hell, I'm not going to live out here.*

The house was decorated in a way that was totally different from anything that Doris and I liked, or came close to liking. There were fake plastic flowers in every available nook and cranny. Semi-religious quotations in overly ornate picture frames were interspersed with photographs of fat babies being held up for the camera or being ridiculously posed with fat adults sporting false smiles and badly fitting clothing. There was a strange perfume in the air and a feeling of claustrophobia wherever one went.

Nothing matched, nothing had anything like our idea of taste, and here we were disrupting these poor folks and maybe even giving them false hope that we were prospective buyers. I felt awful and soon lost interest in the tour. I'd had enough.

Abby showed us the guest rooms, none of which appealed. I was itching to get back on the road.

"Oh, but wait—wait you have to see our dining room," Abby said. "Guests just love our dining room."

And there it was, the dreaded single table—and this one was enormous. This dining table was way too big for the room, and it must have been quite the challenge for anybody to reach and pass anything that had found its way to its center, let alone just maneuver around the outside of the table to find a place to sit.

"Gosh," said Doris. "Where on earth did you find a table like this?"

Abby puffed with pride and said, "Ralph made it. He made it all from scratch. Ralph has made most of the furniture that we have, and he does all the repairs himself, too."

Ralph, who had moved to a chair where he just sat not saying anything, nodded in acknowledgement.

"Now you are just going to be thrilled with the owner's quarters." Abby went on. "We think of it as a bonus to the buyers of the inn."

Abby opened the door to their part of the house, and the first thing that met you was the biggest television screen that you had seen outside of HH Gregg. It completely dominated the room. It commanded that you look at it even, as it was now, turned off. Two small chairs cowered in front of this behemoth.

"We usually eat in the dining room with the guests," Abby said, "except sometimes on a tray in front of the TV."

There was a doorway next to and actually tucked a little way behind the monster screen, which led to the bedroom. Through this door was another, we were told, of Ralph's creations, their bed. He must have made the bed inside the room because there was no way that anything as large as this could have been carried in. Why, I thought, when his wife is only just over five feet tall? All over the ceiling, someone had nailed plastic greenery and brightly colored plastic flowers. The whole setting was almost indescribable, and the wretched perfume still puffed at us.

"I don't know what to say, Abby," I offered.

"Isn't it just beautiful! We just hate to give it up," she replied.

Back in the living room, out of the hearing of the silent Ralph, Alexia whispered to me, "You don't like it, do you."

"It's not that I don't like it, Alexia," I whispered back, "it's just that it has taken my breath away, and I don't know what to say."

"What about your wife?" Alexia asked.

"Don't ask her right now," I said, wanting to protect Alexia from the potential of blasphemy and other bad language from Doris, whose taste I knew well. This was *far* from anything Doris would have liked. "We'll talk about it and let you know."

"You have been very accommodating," I announced to everybody, now that we were all back in the main room. "But Doris and I have to be on our way. This was an unscheduled stop for us."

Alexia, wise beyond her years, quickly responded. "Thank you for coming by. We'll be in touch." Then she gently led us to the front door, smiling all the way, and we made our escape.

"Goodbye," we said, as we left, "and thank you again."

"Goodbye," said Abby. Ralph had still not uttered a single word.

We climbed into the car and were pulling out of the circular drive when I noticed Alexia running down the drive after us. Her magnificent figure was struggling hard to break free from whatever restraints she had tried to put upon it. Again, I was feeling better about stopping here after all.

When she reached the car, I rolled down the window.

"We have other properties, you know," she said, leaning in. "Let me give you my card. I'll be happy to work with you."

"Thanks, Alexia," I replied, as I took her card. "But we've got to get over this one first." We drove off.

"What do you think, Dolly?" I said, once we were out on the freeway.

"What color were Alexia's eyes?" Doris asked me.

"I don't know."

"And...I know why you don't know."

"But the house, Dolly, the inn, what did you think of the inn?"

"Men," she replied. "Why ask? You must know what I think about the inn."

I wanted to remind Doris that she was the reason we had extended the stop over, and Doris was also the reason that Alexia had been summoned to show us around. Bluebell Acres had only been a drive-by on my list. But I thought better of it and pointed the car in the direction of stop number two.

The drive over to Southern Pines was uneventful. We were both trying to absorb our recent experience. It wasn't until we were nearly to our destination that I asked Doris what she thought.

"Well, I have new criteria."

"Oh, that's good. What are your new criteria?"

"No blue ducks. We're not country people. We don't understand country people. We don't want to emulate country people, eat like country people, dress like country people."

"Stop it, Doris," I said, interrupting. "We've always believed in live and let live, and there's a lot about a country way of life that we've enjoyed in the past."

"Name one."

"Subtly spiced—slow cooked in smoke—fall off the bone—succulent—baby back ribs."

"Oh, you and your ribs, and you know that they're not a favorite of mine."

"Hey, here we are at Brookfield House. What do you think?"

"About what? This place looks a lot like Frank Thornton's inn."

"Maybe. Do you want to drive around a little and put it on the list for a future visit? We have only a little time here before we need to make the drive up to Fayetteville, where we have an appointment."

Doris shook her head. "Get Frank Thornton's place out of your mind, Derick, and let's move on to the next stop. No, I don't want to see inside. I feel that I already know what it looks like in there."

"I'm checking it as a 'maybe,'" I said, but I knew that Southern Pines would probably not be featured in our future lives.

I did a little inward soul searching on our drive up to Fayetteville. Doris had slipped into sleep. I really was asking a lot of this poor wife of mine, and if she objected or hesitated every now and then, or if she questioned what on earth was going on, she had every right to do so. Also, had I subconsciously sought out Frank Thornton for advice knowing that he would put a rosy complexion on our endeavor? "Straw Boss and Concierge" can't be all that one needs to know about owning and running a bed and breakfast. What about all of the things about which we knew very little? Occupancy rates, average daily room rate, advertising, making reservations, staff, website, suppliers—the list could be endless, and although Doris must have thought about and worried about all of these areas, I'd just blown them off as easy. And what about worries regarding our lack of experience with even one aspect of running an inn? Here she was going along with my plan of investing all that we had and our entire future in the enterprise. I was going to have to slow down, be a lot nicer to Doris, and more thoughtful of what all this means if I had any hopes to pulling it off.

"Fayetteville," I announced. "Okay, Flo. Direct us to 'The Magnolia House.'"

This woke up Doris.

"What is this one all about?" she asked.

"Well—" *I've got to stop saying "Well" before I start each sentence. I'm beginning to sound like Ronald Regan,* I thought to myself.

"Well! The Magnolia House is a pretty big inn. It has seven bedrooms. It's an antebellum house that looks fabulous in the photographs. Queen Ann style with large curved and flowing lines. It does fantastic business according to its listing. It has been on the market for quite a while, and I think that that is because they are asking for a lot of money. It is one of the most expensive on our list, and I'm not sure that we can swing it. But it is certainly worth consideration. We're going to meet with their real estate agent."

"Not another Alexia, please," was all Doris had to say about that.

"I couldn't get that lucky two times in one day," I replied.

SEMI-RETIREMENT

And then we were there.

It looked fantastic as we drove up the road towards the inn. The street that we were traveling on dead-ended into another road and The Magnolia Inn stood in all its glory at the intersection.

"Wow." It took our breaths away.

As we drew closer, it looked better and better. The outside lights had been switched on, as it was late afternoon. The landscaping was neat and tidy. There was an inviting semi-circular drive in front of the impressive front porch and double door.

We had already pulled into the drive before we saw a discrete sign indicating that the drive was for loading and unloading only, and that parking was in the rear.

Without stopping and getting out of the car, I drove forward in search of the parking lot. I should have turned left out of the drive and driven past the house again to access the parking lot. The Magnolia House was situated on a very large lot, about three acres, almost a square three acres. The house itself was situated in the bottom right corner of the lot with a flower garden to its left and the parking lot, along with other buildings and structures behind. If I had made the left turn, I would have driven past the house and garden again, then easily found the parking lot. But by mistake, I turned right.

A high privet hedge grew along the lot line to the right of the house, and the house was very close to it. On the other side of the hedge was one of the ugliest, most cheaply built strip malls that either of us had ever seen. It was obvious that it had been years since anyone had bothered with any upkeep. There was a convenience grocery, a shoe shop, a dollar store of sorts (not one of the national chains)—all with litter strewn around them. The last store in the mall, the one on the end closest to the inn, was a Chinese take away and restaurant. The restaurant was getting ready for the evening trade, and the aroma of cheap Chinese food had just started to permeate the air.

"Oh no," I said, "I can't deal with this."

"None of this showed up in the pictures online, eh?" asked Doris.

"Doris, I'm so sorry. I had no idea. I'm not even remotely interested, are you?"

"No, not really. What will you do?"

"I'll call the real estate person and tell them it's off." I reached for my cell phone.

"Hello, this is Derick Anderson; we have an appointment to view the inn. Look, I'm sorry, but I didn't know about the mall and restaurant next door. I'm afraid that this is not what we're looking for."

"Where are you calling from?" said the female voice through my cell phone.

"From the parking lot in front of the Chinese take away," I said.

"Well you're here; you might as well come and at least look."

"I don't think so," I said, but Doris was nodding her head at me.

I asked the woman to hold on, and Doris said that as we were here we should go on and look at the place just to gain more experience. I really didn't want to gain more experience this way, but the argument made sense so I took my phone off hold.

"Okay, I'm overruled. We'll be right there."

"I'm going to park in their driveway for a quick get away," I told Doris, as I put the car into drive and retraced our steps.

Again, the inn looked fabulous as we parked outside their front door, but the perfume of Chinatown had gotten into my nostrils and was quite ruining the effect. We were met by Sheila, the real estate agent—short and a tad overweight, quite the opposite of Alexia. Alongside Sheila were Herb and Lauren Royce, owners of The Magnolia House. I hadn't been expecting them.

"Hello," said Sheila, "glad that you changed your mind."

Herb was a tall, impressive looking man who exuded self-confidence. Lauren was an attractive middle-aged woman but obviously the junior partner to Herb. She was smiling, whereas Herb had a serious look on his face.

Without any word of "hello" or welcome of any kind, Herb said, "So, you are interested in buying The Magnolia House."

I wasn't going to be intimidated. "Well," *there I go again with the "well,"* "I was interested in talking about it, but your immediate neighbors have dimmed my enthusiasm, to be frank." I was proud of myself for standing up to him.

"Let me show you around," he said. "And change your mind back to buying the inn."

"Well . . . I . . . um . . . " I was mumbling and losing my authority and should have said "No" and driven away, but Doris spoke up—after all, she was the one who thought that we needed the exposure and practice.

"Yes, show us around please, thank you."

The inn was unbelievably awesome. Herb told us that he had bought an old derelict house and built it into this palace. The furnishings and decorations were tasteful and obviously expensive. Each bedroom had a theme attached to it like *Gone with the Wind* or *Cat on a Hot Tin Roof* and was decorated accordingly. The dining room had individual tables, which were all beautifully set for dinner. I had known that The Magnolia House was also a restaurant but had no idea that that part of its business was as large as it appeared. The kitchen was large and professionally equipped. Everything that we saw was top notch.

Out back, at least half of the lot had been turned over into an outdoor arena with a cement floor and tent-like cover.

Herb explained that this was for functions like weddings and reunions and that they could accommodate up to five hundred people back there for such occasions.

Herb told us his theory for running his business and likened it to a three-legged stool. One leg was the bed and breakfast aspect, another leg was the restaurant, and the third leg was the functions out back. If one leg was experiencing a downturn, then the other two supported it.

Herb added, "I'm serious about this: The Magnolia House would not be able to function without all three legs of the stool."

During the tour and the whole presentation, we saw nothing of Sheila the real estate agent or Lauren, Herb's wife. They had quietly retired to the living room. It was very clear who was in charge.

"Herb," I said, "this whole operation is remarkably impressive. Why are you selling it?"

Herb thought for a while, then looked at me with a steely gaze.

"In addition to running The Magnolia House, I am an ordained minister. I'm telling you in confidence; Lauren is not well, something questionable on her liver. I turned to the Lord for advice and God is telling me to devote less time to The Magnolia House and spend more time with Him and Lauren."

I was stumped for a minute. I knew that I had to find the courage somehow to tell this man that even if God was on his side of the ball, and that I was also sorry for his sick wife, I didn't want to live cheek and jowl next to a Chinese take away. My reasoning seemed paltry compared to his calling and his dedication to his family.

Doris came to my rescue. "This operation is too large for us, Derick," she said. "Remember when we started you said that you didn't want an inn with a restaurant?"

"I thought that if the property was worth it otherwise we would close a restaurant if there was one there already," I told her.

"Then what about Herb's three-legged stool argument that you need all three legs to make this place tick?"

Bingo! She'd trumped him with his own argument, and the Chinese take away didn't need to be brought into play.

"Sorry, Herb." She looked him in the eye. "Too big for us. We don't want a restaurant, and according to you, the business can't run without all three legs."

"At least think about it, won't you?" Herb looked a little taken aback as we made our way to the living room. He must have known that he had been snookered. He must have also figured out that Doris wasn't an easy sell. I'm sure he was working on his next argument when we met the others, so I quickly announced, "We have to leave." I said this with all the authority I could muster, trying to establish my authoritarian role again. "We're going to think about it."

I hustled Doris out of the front door to the waiting car. Both Sheila and Lauren had surprised looks on their faces, and Herb flushed trying desperately to find a way of getting us to stay.

I fired up the car and in no time we were out of there.

"Doris, you were magnificent," I told her.

"I don't believe for a minute that either Lauren is sick or that Herb has daily chats with Jesus," Doris said. "I also don't think for a second that he built that place all by himself. He's not a shyster, that man. I just think that he is delusional and probably believes all that he thinks up. Anyway, he is nobody that we should be doing business with. I bet that it is just impossible to finalize any kind of deal with him—there will always be something or somebody talking in his ear."

"You go, girl," I said, feeling very proud of my wife. "Do you fancy Chinese food tonight?"

"Just get to the hotel," was all that she replied.

Marriott Courtyard. I used to be a big honcho with Marriott when I traveled a lot, but I'm just an ordinary guy off the street with them these days—no more upgrades and complimentary this, complimentary that. However, they do a good enough job, and at least the Courtyards have a bar and small restaurant where one can get a meal with a glass of wine without going out. Doris actually prefers to stay in when we are on the road, and I was tired, so we just checked in, found our room, and unpacked.

We usually travel with our own stash, a small bottle of whisky and small bottle of gin so that we can enjoy an evening cocktail together without bothering to clean up and change, and tonight we ordered room service so didn't have anything to do except crash. Doris really likes her evening cocktail, and she loves room service—and she certainly deserved them after today.

"Any thoughts on today?" I asked.

"Yes. I don't want to go country, and that was confirmed. I don't want a restaurant, and that was confirmed, too. And after seeing you ogle Alexia, I've confirmed that I'm still married to a dirty old man, but I love him."

My cell phone rang. It was Sheila.

"You didn't like The Magnolia House?" she enquired.

"No," I said. "That's not strictly true. We liked it very much. We didn't like the surroundings, but we will think about it. It's also a little more than we are looking for."

"I have other listings," she said. "I would love to work with you."

"We're a little tired, Sheila. Can we have this conversation sometime tomorrow or the next day? I'll call you."

"Sure," she said.

I hung up.

"Bet you'd still be talking if that had been Alexia on the phone," Doris chimed in.

"Oh, Dolly, let's clear our heads and get some rest."

She raised her gin and tonic to that. "Cheers."

CHAPTER 3

Search Day 2

The next morning, we got a good start for our journey down to Athens and a drive-by of the second inn on our list named Magnolia. This inn was in the heart of town.

Athens to us was very appealing, very much the college town. The University of Georgia is evident wherever one goes, and there is a warm, friendly, almost welcoming feeling about the place. Magnolia, on the other hand, was a great disappointment. It was situated near some fraternity houses and whereas frat houses, as one might expect, have that "college kids live here" look about them, Magnolia was worse, very run down.

"This is a shame," I said. "I wonder what the story is about this place."

It was all locked up tight, and there wasn't any response to our knock on the door or shouts of "Anybody home?"

We looked through the windows as best we could, and the place looked just as run down inside as it did out.

"It has potential," Doris noted, "and I like the feel of the town."

"Yes, but the amount of work to bring it up to any kind of standard seems to be staggering and expensive. I wish that there was somebody around."

There was.

Sometimes it's a good thing to have a nosy neighbor, and there she was in the house across the street peeking though a window and, perhaps deliberately, making the curtain move. I waved to her and very shortly she came over.

"If you are looking for somewhere to stay, you won't find much luck here," she said.

"Actually, we're potential buyers," I replied. "I haven't made any appointments, just thought that I'd drive by first and look from the outside, inside too if there was somebody home."

"Nobody here," she said. "The place has been going downhill for over a year now. There was a death, the owner. His wife was left to run the place by herself."

"I'm sorry," I said.

"So was she, and resentful. She started to lose interest after she was left alone and complained that it was hard work for a single person, so she found a manager, whom she brought in to help. He's just a bad lot. He lives here but isn't ever home. Now she has taken to spending more and more time with her sister in Atlanta, and the place is just going downhill."

"But it *is* for sale?" I asked.

"Has been since the day after the funeral," she went on, "but no buyers. Most people come away saying that it would take too much to get it back into shape. Guests have stopped coming, too, except for football weekends in the fall, and they are just trouble with their loud parties and all that drinking."

Doris wanted an end to the conversation. "Thank you," she said. "You *have* been helpful."

The woman wouldn't stop. "Nobody here wants a bed and breakfast in the neighborhood," she said. "There should be a nice family living here—conservative and quiet, like the rest of the families on the street."

"Okay, we've got your message," I said, nodding.

I think that she would have liked to have gone on in greater detail regarding her views of nice families and sinful bed and breakfasts, but Doris and I had retreated into our car. At least we knew where we were not wanted, and at our stage of life, there is no way that we wanted even a skirmish in the war going on in this woman's mind.

We started the car and put it in gear. As we drove out of Athens, Doris said, "It's a pity, you know, I really like this city."

"Time to move on. I wonder what that old witch thinks about the fraternities," I replied. "We can actually get to our next stop early and save some time at the end of the day. Our next stop is just south of Atlanta, not too far from the airport."

The Generals' Quarters looked great, a beautiful federal-style southern plantation house on a large lot of land. Our appointment was for 1:00 PM, but we arrived in town just after 11:30 AM. I was pleased that we were ahead of schedule and all psyched up. I really liked the outside look of the place and wanted to get in to see how it was equipped inside. The door was locked, so I rang the bell. A young man, looking as though he had just woken up after a whole night of partying, came to the door and abruptly, at least that's what I thought, asked what I wanted.

"We are the Andersons," I told him. "We have an appointment to look around at 1:00 PM. We're early."

"It's not even noon," he replied. "You are over an hour early."

"Is that a problem?" I asked.

"Of course it's a problem," he responded. "If you say that you are going to be here at one o'clock and then show up at noon, it's a problem." He was getting quite agitated.

"Well, I'm sorry," I said. "Our earlier appointment didn't last as long as we had thought, so we came straight here."

"That's your problem. That's not my problem," he retorted. "Go away and come back at one."

With that he closed the door, and Doris and I were left standing there with amazed looks on our faces.

"What the hell was that all about?" I asked Doris.

"We came too early," she said. "Some people can't bend."

"Well . . . do you want to come back?"

"Yes," she said. "The inn looks lovely. Why don't we look around the town and find somewhere for lunch."

As much as we loved Athens, this little Georgia town, home of The Generals' Quarters, did nothing for us. Most of the buildings were in disrepair. There were dogs running in the streets, and most of the people that we saw were poorly dressed and seemed to be hunched over as they walked. There were cars, mostly clunkers, parked haphazardly around in no particular order, and all of them were in need of a good wash and a repair or two.

"I don't get this place," I said. "It's depressing."

There were two sandwich shops around the main square; one of them was more bar than restaurant. Neither was particularly busy.

"Fancy either of them?" I asked.

"You know I don't," Doris replied, and I had to agree with her. The depressing ambiance associated with this little town had quite taken my appetite away, not to mention our recent encounter with the guy at The Generals' Quarters.

We just drove around until it was closer to 1:00 PM and then found our way back to the inn. I was obviously intimidated as a result of our recent encounter, so I waited until the big hand passed twelve and the little hand was pointing at one before we parked in the drive and once again rang the doorbell.

This time two young men answered the door together: one, the same fellow with whom we'd had the run-in before; and the other, maybe a little younger, new to us.

Again, I introduced us. "We are the Andersons. I'm Derick, and this is my wife Doris."

"I'm Keith." He was the one to whom we had talked earlier, and he still looked remarkably bedraggled. "This is my partner James."

I didn't know whether to bring up our previous conversation, and as he still had the same belligerent look about him, decided not. He didn't mention it either.

"We're here to look over the inn with the idea of a possible purchase," I went on.

Still no smiles, no charm. Keith almost acted as though he were distant and distracted from this whole encounter, not a part of it whatsoever. James, maybe smiled, but at the same time had an air of sadness about him. I was out of my element here.

"You look around, and if you have questions come and find us," we were directed by Keith. More confusion on my behalf. Did the guy want to sell the place?

"Thank you," Doris replied. "Come on, Derick, let's check it out."

The inn was fabulous. The building was authentic federal style, old, my guess late 1700s early 1800s, and it was decorated with reproduction furniture appropriate to the period. The wall hangings, paintings, and general decorations were tasteful, not too much. Everything was as Doris and I would have wanted it to be had we started from scratch, with sufficient funds. However, we were never quite capable of achieving the final look that had been achieved here. There were six bedrooms, with either king size or queen size beds. The bedrooms were all different from each other but all in keeping with the style and period of the house. Each bedroom had its own bathroom, and all the bathrooms were equipped with two-person Jacuzzi tubs. The appointments in both bedrooms and bathrooms appeared to be of the highest quality—thick towels, expensive soaps, and silky sheets with fluffy comforters. Doris especially was impressed, almost beyond belief.

The common rooms, too, were comfortable and inviting. Unfortunately, the dining room was furnished with a large single table, but we noted that there was plenty of room should we wish to change the configuration to small, individual tables. It was odd to us that in one room probably the music room because there was an old square grand piano there and an ornate gold painted harp next to a sideboard. Overflowing from the sideboard on to a table next to it, was one of the largest collection of all varieties of liquor that I'd ever seen outside a bar or liquor store. Some of the bottles were unopened, but most were half to three quarters full.

The kitchen was nicely organized and well equipped with two of everything—two dishwashers, two ovens, even two sinks in separate parts of the room. There was a large center island that would be very convenient when plating ten to twelve plates at one time.

"Let's talk to them," I said to Doris.

"Do you know what you're going to say? And are you going to get mad?" she wanted to know.

"I'm fine," I replied.

They were sitting in the main parlor.

"Keith, James, your place is beautiful. It must be a difficult decision to have to sell," I said.

No response.

"Who is responsible for the decorations?" I was trying to break the ice.

"I am," Keith replied. "James is the cook, bottle washer, and handy man around the house. He is very particular about where the different items get placed on the plates. I keep the books and look after all things business."

"All things business," I repeated with a smile, still trying to lighten things up.

He stared at me coldly, waited a few seconds, then said very slowly, "From soup to nuts." I could feel the freeze.

Doris asked about the owner's quarters, and we were informed that that would be a separate negotiation and not included in the asking price for the inn.

"Where is it?" she persisted.

"Out back," Keith replied, "but we usually spend our nights in one or other of the guest rooms in the inn."

"Oh."

I wanted to know about the liquor collection.

"Our guests often travel great distances and are too tired to go out after they arrive, so we provide an open bar for their convenience," Keith said. However, my guess was that there wasn't anywhere to go in the depressing town anyway.

"Where do most of your guests come from?" I asked.

"Mostly Atlanta," Keith answered. "We get flight crews on layover at the airport."

"Asking price firm?" I enquired.

"One million," he replied.

"And the owner's quarters?" I went on.

"You can have that for two thousand." Keith was beginning to get fed up with me, and I for sure was getting fed up with him.

Doris sensed our moods. "Can we at least see the owner's quarters?" she asked.

"No," said Keith. "Not without an appointment." But then James jumped into the conversation.

"It's the house trailer just past the large oak in the back yard," James said.

Keith turned to him and gave him a look that would have frozen molten rock. I didn't want to be in James's shoes at that moment.

"No more questions. Shall we go?" I asked Doris, and she readily agreed.

"Thank you both," I said to our hosts, as we made for the door.

"The next time you make an appointment for 1:00 PM, show up for the appointment at 1:00 PM," was Keith's parting remark.

We said nothing, and I almost stumbled as we passed through the front door.

"Are you all right?" asked Doris.

"I will be when this place is out of our rear view mirror," I replied.

Into the car, gear lever into drive, squeeze on the accelerator, and thankful for the noise that tires make as we crunched down the drive.

"Put your seat belt on," commanded Doris.

"How about a flack jacket, too," I said. "I bet he has a large selection of weaponry back there and is probably now looking for something appropriate, with us as his target."

We rode in silence for a while until I heard what sounded like a chuckle coming from Doris's direction. Soon the chuckle had turned into prolonged heaving, then full-blown laughter.

"Wait until I tell the children." Doris was still laughing. "Alec especially is so homophobic he's going to really enjoy hearing about how his father went down to Georgia to buy an inn from a couple of gay men. And the way dear old Dad handled the situation, getting mad, almost unable to control his temper. Then the retreat down the driveway with squeaking wheels and gravel flying all around...."

"Dolly," I took a deep breath. "Do you want to live there?"

More laughter and convulsive heaving. "Oh yes. I really want to live in a single wide in a dismal looking town in the deep south. That's always been an aspiration of mine. I did like the inn though."

"Dolly, I'm sorry."

More laughter. "Oh, don't be sorry. I wouldn't have missed the last few hours for anything. What have you got up your sleeve for our next stop?"

"Next stop is just a drive-by and not too far from here. Maybe if it doesn't look viable we'll just drive on home tonight."

"You go, guy." She was calming down.

Still south of Atlanta but now east of Interstate 75, we found the Old Doctor's House in another unfortunate run-down town. Neither of us had any idea that Georgia had such contrasting cities. Some of the towns we drove through looked idyllic—neat, tidy, well-kept homes—while others contrasted by being dirty, untidy, and depressed. It was unfortunate that the inns we had planned to look at, with the exception of Athens, were in the poorer towns.

This time however, the Old Doctor's House more fitted its surroundings than did The Generals' Quarters. This inn needed help. It showed a weathered look and was in desperate need of a good coat of paint. It stood on a street corner downtown and had virtually no yard around it. It just didn't look good.

"What do you think?" I asked.

"What do I think?" Doris replied. "How about," and she started to sing, "Hit the road Jack, and don't you come back no more, no more, no more, no more. Hit the road Jack…. Didn't Ray Charles also sing, 'Georgia on my mind'?" Doris asked

"Probably. He was from Georgia, wasn't he?" I mumbled.

"Don't know. How long will it be before we get home?"

"Well after dark," I replied. "Are you up for it?"

"Oh yes," she said. "Home, James, and don't spare the horses."

I reset Flo and pointed the car back to our island.

The next morning, we awoke to find that work on killing the greens to make them greener had begun. The seventeenth out back was already several shades of yellow on to brown on to black; there was almost no green color left. Somewhat symbolic, I thought. The weather reporter was also nattering on about a depression that had formed in the Atlantic, which eventually had the potential of causing much disaster and doom. They went on to describe, in vivid detail, all the disaster and doom caused by previous storms, which they did when each new potential for a depression or storm was identified.

"They've got to keep us informed," Doris said. However, I knew that she was uncomfortable, and I had to remind myself that when I'd originally sold Doris on the idea of living on the coast, I'd promised that we would move inland at even the hint of bad weather. We had a day or two before we needed to be on the road again, and I was hoping that the current danger would find its way into the Gulf of Mexico and leave the Atlantic alone.

We relaxed, saying little about our search so far. There wasn't much to discuss. We didn't like the country place; Southern Pines was still a potential in my mind, but Doris was put off because it seemed too much like Frank Thornton's place, and she had a thorn in her side about Frank Thornton. The Magnolia House was too much for us; Magnolia in Athens was a bust. The Generals' Quarters and the Old Doctor's House were in completely unacceptable surroundings and had been ruled out by both of us. Nothing to do really but get some rest and get ready for the next foray.

"We'll drive up the coast to New Bern and check The Captain's Retreat," I told Doris, "and then cut across to Leesburg to check out Harmony Hotel. We'll spend the night in Roanoke, drive over to Blacksburg, and check out the inn there before heading to West Virginia where we're booked into Preston Hall.

"After that, we're about through with our first round. We will drive by Historic Primrose Inn on our way to Columbus, but as far as I can determine it doesn't fit well with our original criteria."

"Good," said Doris. "I'm looking forward to seeing the children again."

The bags got packed, the car made ready again, Flo was programmed, and we were ready for the next round. The nagging storm was still threatening. It had not turned toward the Gulf, as I had hoped, but was dancing around still in the Atlantic trying to make up its mind where to hit land. The storm had drifted north of South Carolina, and there was still no clear indication of where it was heading.

I put several of Doris's favorite CDs in the car in an attempt to divert her from wanting to listen to the radio and weather reports as we drove north.

Early morning, and we did well to get through Charleston before rush hour. The road north out of the city, Highway 17, was straight and mostly divided. We had been on this route to Myrtle Beach on several prior occasions, so we knew the journey quite well. All was uneventful until we got through Myrtle Beach and I turned on the radio for an update. "Clarence," now a named storm, had gotten its act together and by some uncanny act of the devil had decided to follow us up Highway 17. The weatherman said that Clarence, if he stayed on his current course, would most likely make landfall near a town called New Bern. Warnings had been issued, and folks had begun to invade the supermarkets and hardware stores.

"Where is it that we're going?" Doris asked.

"New Bern."

"Did you just hear what they said on the radio?" she said, getting agitated and looking at me with Betty Davis eyes.

"Oh, we'll be out of there long before any storms hit land," I said. "It's a short visit."

"No!! You don't get it, Derick," she said, shaking her head. "I don't care about this visit. This visit isn't going to happen anyway. What you need to understand is that I don't want to live again in a town that every now and then gets mentioned as a place where you have to take cover because all hell is going to break loose."

I had no answer.

"Get them on the phone and tell them 'no deal.' They'll understand. They've probably left themselves if they have any sense. Program Flo for the next stop, and it had better be a left turn out of the way of Clarence."

When Doris gets into these sorts of moods and starts speaking in statements, I have no choice but to listen. Anyway, I couldn't help but agree with her. Pushing on to New Bern was both foolish, with all the traffic coming in the opposite direction, and futile—we weren't going to live there ever.

The call was made, and actually they *didn't* understand. A storm every couple of years to them was acceptable. But the decision was firm, and The Captain's Quarters were informed that it was final. The car was rerouted, and we were now on our way to Leesburg. We were going to be early.

We found ourselves in another delightful small town. Leesburg has two universities, an historic downtown, interesting shops, and seemingly eclectic restaurants. What diversity this country is, I thought, and what a pleasant surprise to find Leesburg.

We drove around and easily came across Harmony Hotel. It was right there on the main street. We were early, and I was reluctant for a repeat of our previous experience when we'd arrived before expected. Doris understood.

There was nothing outstanding about Harmony Hotel; it looked very much like an ordinary house on a street of ordinary houses and nothing like an inn. There was a sign in the yard, or we would have had trouble identifying it.

"How about if we drive around and find somewhere for a snack?" I suggested.

SEMI-RETIREMENT

As we drove past, I noticed a woman sweeping the pathway that led from the sidewalk to the front door of Harmony Hotel. She was very diligent. We didn't stop but drove into town and found a sandwich bar. Our waitress was friendly, a college student, and the food was good and fresh as a daisy.

"I like this, Doris," I said.

"Good, so do I."

We still had time before our appointment, so we decided to scope out the immediate area around the inn. The same woman was still sweeping; it must have been nearly an hour since we'd seen her before. Now she was working on the city sidewalk, sweeping and sweeping. I was at a loss to understand why. I slowed the car down and opened the window as we passed by. I thought that I could hear a piano being played in the background coming from within the house. The music sounded like a hymn, very loud and not very well played. We drove around to the back where the contrast to the front was staggering. Whereas the front of the house had a nice, albeit small, well-kept yard—plus the cleanest walkway in town—the back, by contrast, was stark and ugly. Really, it was just a place where cars were parked, with no attempt at landscaping or tidiness or anything whatsoever. There was a low chain link fence along the property line, and a man in the yard of the house next door was cooking away on his barbeque grill. He was making a lot of smoke, and perhaps that is why he had taken his shirt off. Probably he was getting hot even though we were now into fall. Not only was there smoke from his grill, but he was also doing an admirable job of smoking up the neighborhood with the fat cigar stuffed in the right side of his mouth.

"Now there is a sight that you don't want to see everyday," announced Doris.

"Especially next to one's prospective home," I added.

"Dream on," Doris said.

It was time. We parked on the main road so as to avoid the barbeque action and a possible conversation with the guy next door. We walked up the clean pathway and knocked on the door, which was opened by the sweeping lady.

"We're the Andersons," I said.

She smiled. "Please come in. I'll call my husband."

Duane and Elenoretta were the owners of Harmony House. He was tall, thin, and middle-aged, with a full head of thick and graying hair. She was shorter and had more weight on her than had seemed when she was out sweeping the sidewalk. Both were dressed conservatively, with dark and old-fashioned looking clothing.

"We're blessed to meet you," he announced, shaking hands with us.

Elenoretta just smiled.

Duane was obviously the man in charge.

"So, the Lord has directed you here to buy the inn." It was more a statement than a question.

I tried to make light of what he'd just said by replying that our GPS Flo had directed us here, and at this stage, we were only looking things over.

Duane was not impressed.

"We will show you around." He pointed out a very small living room just off the very small hall, a very small dining room—again, with one community table—also off the hall, and a narrow staircase leading up to the next floor.

There were three small bedrooms, none with more than a double bed, and all were somewhat sparsely furnished compared to bedrooms we had seen in other inns. There was only one toilet, so we presumed, without asking, that everybody had to share.

Back downstairs we were led through the dining room into a surprisingly large kitchen. It sported a wood burning pot bellied stove and two reclining arm chairs.

"We spend quite a lot of our time in this room," Duane informed us.

The owner's bedroom was situated off the kitchen and was also a room of decent proportions. There was a queen size bed, two chests of drawers, and an upright piano. I asked Duane if he was the pianist, and he confirmed that he did play. There was a hymnal open on the music rack.

"Now for our secret room," Duane said, as he led us through another door off the kitchen and down some very steep basement steps.

Doris balked. "I'm not going down there," she said.

"You must!" Duane commanded.

"No, I don't must," Doris answered sharply.

I could tell that he was taken aback.

I alone followed Duane to the bottom of the steep staircase. Piled around, in no particular order, at the bottom of the stairs were heaps of broken down furniture, which Duane described as antiques that he was holding onto for resale. We squeezed past the piles of furniture to where a curtain was hung from one side of the basement to the other. Behind the curtain, which he pulled to one side, was another full size bed all made up and ready for the evening.

"When we're busy," he explained, "we rent our room upstairs and we sleep down here."

"Okay," I said, "let's get back." I wasn't impressed, and I nearly tripped on the steep stairway back up into the kitchen. Duane followed.

"Questions?" Duane asked, once we'd rejoined Doris. "Come, let's join hands and pray that we successfully navigate the Anderson's course in becoming the new owners of Harmony House."

We went into the small living room, and I asked Elenoretta aside and out of hearing of Duane if she minded the times when she had to sleep in the basement.

"We sleep there all the time," she answered.

"I'm sorry. I thought that you only went down there when the inn was full?"

"No, that's our room."

Duane heard the end of our exchange, and he glared at her.

It is difficult when you know that you have no interest in buying an inn but you have actually witnessed trouble being taken on your behalf in getting it ready for you to see it. So rather than say, "Sorry, not interested," I asked questions. Besides, I was feeling sorry for Elenoretta, as she was the one who had done all the sweeping up.

"What is your occupancy rate?" I asked, trying to sound as if I knew what I was taking about.

"$50.00 or so a night," answered Elenoretta.

"No, the percentage rate of how many guests you have staying per night."

"What?" She looked puzzled.

"Well..." I went on. "If every room is full, that would be one hundred percent. If only half the rooms have people in them, that would be fifty percent, and then you average that out over time," I was surprising myself that I was making some sense.

Elenoretta shrugged. "When there is something going on in the colleges, we have people staying here. When they are quiet, we do not have people staying here."

I wasn't getting anywhere. "How about your average daily rate?" I asked.

"Show the man the books, Elenoretta." This came from Duane, who it seemed had tried to get into the conversation before but had been beaten by answers from Elenoratte before he had a chance to speak.

Elenoretta left, and Duane leaned over toward us. "She keeps all the paperwork, so I let her answer your questions."

I was beginning to think that neither of them knew what they were doing.

Elenoretta came back with a small, spiral bound notebook and some supermarket receipts held under a paperclip. She opened the book and showed us a column of figures that meant nothing, and I was not inclined to embarrass her further by asking for an explanation.

I tried to fake it for Elenoretta's sake. "Which are the taxes?" I asked.

"Taxes?"

"Taxes woman!" Duane almost shouted at her. "The taxes that we pay to the government."

"But we don't," she replied. I was so embarrassed for Elenoretta.

"Okay," I said, changing the subject, "then tell us, why are you selling the place?"

"I've been called," Duane said, swelling up.

Not again, I thought. *Not another religious calling.* What is it about the bed and breakfast industry that attracts these sorts of people and this behavior? I wondered.

"I've been called to spread the word and convert and succor the heathen. We are prepared to pass up this wonderful life here in Leesburg to travel into the unknown and spread the word of God. Praise him."

"Praise him," Elenoretta added.

"Will you help me, brother?" Duane said. He stared right into my eyes.

"Don't know about that right now," I mumbled, "but thank you for your time, Duane. Doris and I must be on our way. You've given us enough to think about for one day."

"Praise be, praise be," Duane said. "When can we hear back from you?"

"Duane, we need to consider all that you've told us and seek advice. I'm sure that you know what I mean."

"Praise be," he repeated. "I'll be praying for you, brother. I'll be asking Him to guide your steps back to this door. You will be in our thoughts and in our prayers."

"Praise him, praise him." This was Elenoretta in the background.

We let ourselves out.

Back in the car, Doris looked at me. "We're batting even on the religious freaks, you and me," she said. "What little gems have you found for us next?"

"I feel sorry for that woman," I said.

"Yes, so do I," Doris replied. "But she chose to be the doormat, and it's nothing to do with us if that is the way she wants to live. Apart from all that, you really expect me to sleep in a basement and spend my evenings in front of a pot bellied stove, do you?"

"Doris, I feel a calling coming on. I feel moved to tell you about this revelation that I've had . . . I—"

She interrupted me. "Get on to the hotel, Reverend! It's Miller time. And mine's a G. and T."

Another quiet night, another Courtyard Inn.

CHAPTER 4

Search Day 3

Our appointment at Mountainside Inn in Blacksburg was late enough in the morning to allow us time to drive around and get the feel of another delightful college town. Well kept from the outside, we liked the look of Mountainside Inn, although the name was a stretch. The inn was situated near the center of town, and one would be hard pressed to see mountains. The building was old, and maybe one day in the past a mountain could be seen through one of its windows—before the town grew up around it.

"I'm getting a good feeling about this place," Doris said, as we walked through a small but well cared for garden to the front door. The parking lot was to the back and side of the inn, so we had a good look at the building and the yard as we passed through it.

We knocked, and the door was almost immediately answered by a jovial older gentleman who obviously hadn't missed too many calls to the dinner table during his life.

"Are you the Andersons?" he asked, as he pulled the door open.

"We are," I replied.

"Then come on in." The big smile didn't leave his face for a second.

Inside, the house was decorated in a style more modern than any of the inns we had seen up to this point. There was a small reception hallway with a staircase leading off to the left, and on the right was an open double glass doorway leading into a comfortable looking living room. The furnishings were plush and well coordinated in yellow, brown, and a subtle green; it was a pleasing effect. Another glass double door half of the way down the left side of the living room opened into the dining room, and through there was an all-weather glass-enclosed porch. We noted that although the dining room was equipped with a large single table, the porch was set up with many individual tables, seating two to four at each. Both Doris and I, we discovered later, thought it odd that there were so many tables for what was only a small inn with five bedrooms.

Overriding our pleasure at the overall feel and look of the common rooms in the inn was a heavenly aroma wafting out of the kitchen. Somebody in there was creating magic.

We hadn't forgotten our new jovial companion; we were just blown away with all that we were seeing and smelling.

"I'm Billy Schaeffer," he said, "friendly local real estate agent."

"Hello Billy," I answered. "Doris and Derick Anderson. We weren't expecting a real estate guy."

"I know," he said, "but I'm a long time friend of Alice, and she asked me to help out."

"Would that be Alice making the house come alive with whatever is going on in the oven?" Doris wanted to know.

"It would." The smile still hadn't left his face.

"Let me show you around," Billy said. "And later we can go over the numbers. Oh and let me explain, both Alice and I are ex-faculty from the university; we were both in the chemistry department. After we retired, I went into real estate and

Alice went into the bed and breakfast plus catering business. She has a real talent for it."

We were standing in the enclosed all-weather porch. "You've seen the reception area and the main sitting room," Billy said. "And you will notice that we have two dining rooms. One, the original inside room, is only used as an overflow or if we cater a small party. Mostly the porch is used."

"Why so many tables?" I asked.

"Catering," Billy replied. "Alice is held in high regard by the folks across the street at the university, and she attracts a goodly amount of catering contracts. Plus she knows her way around the billing and invoicing, so can often quote at less than the kitchen in the school. This saves the department money, there is way less paperwork, and the food is better. Everybody benefits, including the school kitchen, which doesn't like to cater private faculty events anyway."

"Alice!" Billy shouted through a doorway off the original dining room that led to the kitchen. "The Andersons are here. I'm going to show them around."

A pleasant looking middle-aged woman poked her head around the door, nodded, and sent a smile in our direction.

"I'll join you soon," she called out.

We went back through the living room to the reception hall and followed Billy up the stairs. On the first floor, there were three bedrooms—one quite large and the other two of adequate size. The large room had a king size bed and its own bathroom; the other two rooms, both with queen size beds, had to share a single bathroom between them. As with the downstairs, the rooms were tastefully furnished, clean, and inviting.

Billy then led us up a second flight of stairs where there were two smaller rooms, again beautifully furnished and decorated. These rooms also had to share a small single bathroom.

"It's a shame that there are not more private baths," I commented.

Billy agreed. "Just not enough space," he explained. "The house was not built to be a bed and breakfast."

"One more stop while we're up here." Billy opened a door in the hallway between the two bedrooms and revealed another flight of stairs going up. This stairway was quite steep compared to the others, and Billy struggled a little as he made his way. We followed, and at the top found ourselves in an attic room so close to the roof that we could only stand upright in the center.

"This is Alice's room."

The attic was long and narrow, with a window at one end, a double bed under the eves, and small sitting area, with a comfortable looking chair and side table. There was one small chest of drawers but no closets. Clothing was hanging from racks and looked to be in the way, but the racks couldn't be pushed closer against the sloping ceiling. Behind us on the other side of the opening in the floor where the steps emerged was a curtain, behind which we discovered was a toilet, washbasin, and tiny shower not unlike the showers one finds that have been added to older homes in Europe.

I looked at Doris, and she returned my glance. Billy noticed.

"Of course, you could always use one of the bedrooms on the floor below," he said.

"Wouldn't that mean sharing the bathroom with guests?" asked Doris.

"Close off the floor," Billy suggested.

"Leaving how many rooms?" I asked.

"Four, including this room."

"Would that mean that guests staying in the attic here would have to pass through our quarters?" We were getting nowhere.

To Billy's credit, he didn't pursue the matter, and the three of us filed back down the two staircases.

Alice was waiting for us in the reception area.

"Would you like to see the kitchen?" she asked.

"Alice, we would feel guilty about taking your time," I answered, and then felt guilty myself about not asking Doris if she wanted to continue with the tour.

"We're sorry, Alice," Doris said. "You have a lovely inn, but it is just not what we're looking for. I'm sorry."

"Don't want to sleep in an attic, eh?" Alice asked.

"That's right, and I really don't think that I could keep up with your catering prowess—that must be a lot of work." Doris was getting into it now. "Why are you selling the business?"

"Oh, I'm tired," Alice said. "I can't seem to find time off. I'm by myself, and really it takes two to do what I'm doing."

"I understand, but honestly this is just not what we are looking for." Doris had real empathy in her voice, and I know that she genuinely felt sorry for Alice. "Good luck. We wish you well."

Alice returned Doris's smile with a look of understanding on her face. She looked as if she wanted to say something, but Billy talked first so she turned and returned to the kitchen.

"We appreciate you stopping by," Billy said, as we headed toward the door.

"It was close, Billy," I answered. "The place is in great shape. I'm sure that the right person will come along."

"Got to keep hoping," Billy said, nodding. "I'm the one who is trying to get Alice out of the business. "I'm trying to talk her into marrying me, but she keeps saying that she's too busy."

"She is," Doris said.

"Of course, I would be of no help around here. Both she and I know that," Billy added.

We said our goodbyes and walked back around the pretty pathway to our car. One last look at Mountainside Inn, then back on the road, this time to West Virginia.

"You know, that came close. That inn was one of your better picks," Doris said, as we drove out of town. "Where are we off to now?"

"Preston Hall. It's a little bit of a drive, but we will probably get there early."

"You don't mind if I nap?" Doris reclined the passenger seat as far as it would go. "You can play your music, but not too loud."

It was a pleasant drive through beautiful countryside, and I was trying to sum up everything in my head as we drove along. I listened to the Beatles *Help* album, and was quite relaxed, but I was also coming to the conclusion that my first list of potentials was not coming through for us. I wanted to talk to Doris but didn't want to disturb her. It would have to wait. *Maybe a good thing,* I told myself, *in that it gives me a chance to have my thoughts organized before the two of us have that discussion.*

We were heading west on Interstate 64 and getting close to our exit. It was very rural here. Flo was quiet, and there was very little on her map except for the one road on which we were traveling. It was a little mesmerizing, and I was shocked when we came across our exit and I had to pull off the freeway. We were still, at least I thought, deep into the countryside. According to Flo, we only had a few miles on some back roads before we reached Preston Hall. It was 3:45 PM, and we are about an hour ahead of our schedule.

Doris woke up and, looking around, she saw nothing but trees and an occasional gatepost leading into a field.

"Where are we?"

"Nearly there."

"No. Where are we?"

"West Virginia."

"Derick, where in the hell are we?"

"West-by God-Virginia. Look, Doris, this is just a stop on our way. They don't know that we are in the market to buy a bed and breakfast. It's just a place where we have a reservation to spend the night."

"Derick."

"Okay, maybe I do have some interest. The history of the place is fascinating and very Brit. A son of Lord Preston came here just before the revolution. Maybe he was an outcast from the family, and he built a life and a home for himself in what was then the wilderness."

"What was then the wilderness?" Doris said, interrupting. "What do you call it now?"

"Beautiful," I replied.

"Can't you cancel and we'll drive on to Ohio, where people live in towns and cities where there are buildings and restaurants and shops?"

"No, we're nearly there now, and who knows—you might just fall in love with the place. It is very cheap, and there is a lot of land that goes with the inn."

With that, we came to a small sign pointing us down a dirt road. The sign said "Preston Hall," with an arrow—that was all.

As we emerged from the tree-lined track, there was some open land and a monstrosity of a house standing all alone in an open space. It was like driving into a scene from a gothic horror movie. The house looked every bit like a haunted house, not unlike the house in the movie *Psycho* but more gothic in design, with a steep roofline and tall, thin windows. Preston Hall was built out of a dark grey brick, which had darkened even more over time. There was a slate roof, also dark grey. The place looked to be in very poor repair—one good puff of wind, and it would be reduced to a pile of rubble.

To the front was a poor excuse of a formal English garden, rectangular in shape, poorly stocked, and not well kept. Overgrown, weeds very much in evidence, and the grass in need of a good trim. There was another small sign next to the track on which we were driving, indicating where to park, and yet another sign directing the way to the front door.

We parked and said nothing as we made our way to the house entrance. We approached the gothic entry porch and confronted a small double door, tightly locked.

"Ring the bell," Doris said. "Or better yet, turn around and walk away."

I rang the bell.

No response, so I rang the bell again.

"This is a blessing," Doris said. "The place has been abandoned. Let's get out of here."

But we heard noise, and the door was opened by a thin, angry-looking woman.

She said nothing, just glared at us, so I made the introductions. "We're the Andersons," I said. "We have a reservation."

"You said that you would be here at five o'clock," she responded. "It has only now just passed four."

"Is that a problem?" I enquired.

"Not today," she answered, leaving us bewildered about these inn keepers and their problems with guests arriving early. In this case, she didn't even know that we were in the market to buy an inn; we were paying guests. There was no additional clean up and tidying to be done to attract potential purchasers.

She invited us through the entry door into a small hallway. "Credit card, please," she said.

"Oh, you prefer that we pay when we check in." I was a little taken aback.

"Yes," this woman had all the charm of a flat balloon.

I handed her my card, which she processed.

"You will be in 'Harriet's Room,'" she told us. "That is upstairs on the right. Breakfast is served promptly at eight thirty."

She handed us a well worn sheet of paper on which was a short list of breakfast entrées. "You have to both pick the same," she added.

"Eggs Rellano," I said, looking toward Doris for confirmation. She was staring at me out of a cold, expressionless face. "Yes, Eggs Rellano will be just fine," I concluded.

I handed the woman her piece of paper, and she handed me the key to our room. Not another word was spoken, and she left.

The house was cheaply furnished; an attempt had been made to decorate it in the style of the late seventeen hundreds but had failed miserably because of the quality of the furnishings. It was also sparsely furnished. Maybe this is what Lord Preston's son preferred, but I thought not. The stairs creaked as we ascended to our room, and when there it offered very little in the way of comfort. We had noticed a sign on the banister as we climbed the stairs indicating that we should not put weight on it, and there were several signs in the room directing that we not open the windows, another that we not touch the thermostat. One sign said that said soft drinks were available for purchase but ice was free. There was a small refrigerator off an upstairs hall.

"Tell me again what we are doing here?" Doris said.

"Oh Dolly, I'm sorry, but I wanted to check it out. There is the Brit connection to Lord Preston, a lot of acreage comes with the property, and the asking price is very reasonable."

"Didn't we say something about no mountain tops?"

"We did."

"Didn't we say something about not being too far out in the country?"

"We did."

"Didn't we say something about no creepy old houses that were close to falling down?"

"Dolly, I'm sorry. Let me fix you a drink."

"Big one. What are we going to do about food out here in the wilderness?"

"Oh, I thought I'd shoot myself a deer or maybe trap a rabbit. I'll build a fire. On the other hand, I thought that maybe we'd just truck into town and eat at a restaurant."

"What town?"

"Good question."

Not wanting another encounter with our landlady, we decided to leave quietly and find somewhere for an evening meal. And, as with most things, Doris was right. There were very few signs of civilization as we backtracked our way to the Interstate exit that we had taken to get to Preston Hall. From there, according to Flo, if we took the freeway back to the previous exit, we would find several places to eat. Back on the freeway and five miles later, we were at a place that had some brightly lit usual fast food restaurants and, to our delight, an Applebee's.

We pulled into the parking lot of what looked like a new construction and made our way into the building. The staff were all young, all scrubbed to a shiny clean, and all with smiles on their faces. Our waiter was the cheeriest of all and went by the name of Brent.

"What can I start you off with?" chirped Brent, the smile never leaving his face.

"Where is everybody? It's just past six thirty?" I asked, as there were very few patrons in the restaurant.

"Well, the restaurant here is new," Brent explained. "Folks just don't know we're here, or don't think of us yet when they're looking for somewhere to eat. We are getting more and more folks stopping from the freeway though. Are you passing through?"

"Yes." Doris was quick with her answer.

"But," I said, "we are thinking of moving here."

"Why?" Brent wanted to know. "Everyone else already here is looking to move away."

"Take no notice of him," Doris added. "There is no way that we will be living here, but we *are* hungry."

We ordered, and Brent went off to get our food.

"We need to talk, Derick." Doris looked at me while we waited to be served. "Where is all this taking us? You must promise that there will be no more of these ridiculous stops, or I'm not coming!"

"I know," I said. "This stop was a mistake, but you're right. We do need to assess where we stand with the other places."

The food was good. Brent was cheerful, and the restaurant was quiet so provided an excellent environment and opportunity for us to catch up and review where we had been. We talked throughout a good and tasty meal, for which I was grateful. Doris could have easily been put off as a result of our Preston Hall experience, and we weren't through yet with that one either.

"Okay, Bluebell Acres, the country place."

"No."

"Southern Pines."

"No."

"Fayetteville."

"No."

"Any of them?"

"Not yet." Doris wasn't being hard to please; she was just being honest.

"Southern Pines had potential," I said.

"That's because it's a lot like Frank Thornton's, and I've told you that neither would be good for me."

"Well, there is only one left on our first list. And I have to tell you, Dolly, from the photographs it has a look quite similar to where we're staying tonight. Gothic, but it is not in the country—Historic Primrose Inn is in a town."

"What town?" Doris asked.

"Versailles, Kentucky," I replied.

"Have you ever been there?"

I shook my head no. "I've been to Lexington quite a lot when I was working on the Tricom project, but I've never been to Versailles. By the way, they pronounce it Ver-sales and not Ver-sigh."

"Oh Derick, what are you doing to me. Do we have to go there?"

"We don't have to do anything that you don't want to do, and it is on the list only as a drive-by; we have no appointment. It is also pricy. But it is sort of on our way to Ohio if we take the long way."

"We'll go," Doris said, sighing. "After all, we've got to do something."

We didn't spend a good night at Preston Hall. We concluded that we were the only guests, there were no other cars in their parking area, but we did think that we heard a motor at some time during the night.

"There's probably a sign somewhere that says once you are in for the night you can't go out again," Doris said, when I asked her if she wanted me to investigate the noise.

We were early for breakfast, and we were the only people in the dining room. Again, very sparsely and cheaply furnished. Even though we were early, our food was not. It wasn't until well past eight thirty before a new woman came through with some coffee.

"Just the two of us here this morning?" I asked, trying to be cheerful.

"Just you two," she replied, and tried to smile at us. "I'll have the entrées out in just a moment."

I found the food to be quite acceptable and was pleasantly surprised, but Doris only picked at hers. This new woman hovered a little, as if she was anticipating a question, so I tried to engage her in conversation.

"We didn't meet you last night," I said.

"No, you met Melissa. Melissa and I run the place between us."

"What is it like running a bed and breakfast?" I hoped to pick up some insights about our newly chosen way of life.

"Well, it's not all as glamorous as some people seem to think, and we've had some bad luck recently, which hasn't helped our situation here."

"I'm sorry." Even though I had no right in the world, I was curious. "What happened?" I asked.

"There were four of us," she explained. "Melissa, myself, Bob, and Elsie. We bought the place at a great price when we, well Melissa, me, and Bob, completed our time in the Air Force. We were going to fix it up, upgrade everything, and turn it into a resort spa. No sooner had we got here than Elsie's mother suffered a stroke and Bob and Elsie had to move back to Colorado. Melissa and I bought them out, but it is proving too much for two women to do just by themselves."

"Have you got it up for sale then?" I asked, as if I didn't already know.

"Oh yes, and we've sold it three times now, but financing always seems to fall through. Some folks want us to finance them instead of the bank, but we can't afford that."

"You poor things," added Doris, who was coming around and seemingly full of sympathy.

We finished our breakfast and got ready to leave. I had already loaded our bags into the car. I think that the woman was feeling sorry for us and embarrassed about what had obviously been a poor experience at her inn.

"You know, it affects everything, when you're not happy in what you do. Melissa can be so difficult."

We were on our way out of the dining room headed to the front door.

"We can tell. Good luck to both of you. I believe that I've already paid," I added to the conversation.

She nodded.

"Well thank you, goodbye."

We passed through the door, crossed over to the parking lot, climbed into the car, and were again back on the track—first the side road, then the freeway, and from there west on I-64 towards Kentucky.

"I'm not stopping at any more places like that." Doris was adamant.

I had no hope and no expectation of pleasing even myself, let alone Doris with our drive-by of Historic Primrose Inn. The photographs had it looking very much like Preston Hall. Even though it was described as being within the city limits, the city was only a small town in Kentucky. Add to this, they were asking for a lot of money for an inn of its size. The books were going to have to look really good—if we even get that far.

It was not an unpleasant drive, and as we approached Lexington, the mountains and steep hillsides gave way to gently sweeping hills populated with horse farms—some with black or white painted fences and some with dry stone walls.

I remembered Lexington quite well from when I'd visited to work in the Cancer Center at the University of Kentucky. I'd worked as a monitor subcontracted by Tricom Corporation on a new cancer drug that was in clinical trials. I liked Lexington, but I had never driven out of the city very much, and I don't think that I ever visited Versailles. The airport was on the west side of Lexington, and so was Versailles, so I had a rough idea of where to go.

We stopped in Lexington for lunch. I found a delightful small Italian restaurant that I'd remembered from previous visits. The food was excellent, and we treated ourselves to a noonday glass of wine. Both Doris and I were feeling good when we got back into the car. The weather was pleasant, and we were filled with pasta and Chianti. We headed for the road to Versailles hoping that it wasn't going to take us far out of our way, as we were anxious to get on to Ohio. More horse farms, more painted fences, more dry stone walls, more beautiful scenery—more than anything that I remembered. There had been a lot of tobacco fields in my recollection, but now it seemed that horse farms prevailed.

We found Highway 60 and drove west, enjoying the drive and the day. When suddenly, without warning, we came across an amazing sight on the right-hand side of the road. There was a castle. Even after blinking and shaking our heads, there was still a castle. It was perched on top of a little hill, and there appeared to be construction going on in and around it.

We had seen a lot of castles growing up in England but nothing quite like this. It was very symmetrical, with turrets on each corner, and looked for the world as if it had leaped out of the pages of a children's book.

"What on earth is that?" asked Doris. "Does Mickey Mouse live here? It looks like something out of a Walt Disney movie."

"Probably Mickey is alive and well in there," I answered. "And with our luck, Goofy lives in Historic Primrose Inn." How could I have known?

"Are you sure that we're doing the right thing?" Doris wanted to know. "If people here build fantasy castles on hills, is this really the place where we want to live?"

"The rest of the scenery around here is out-of-your-mind beautiful," I replied. "That thing is the only blot on the landscape, and it's not so bad. Anyway, I think it's funny."

After passing the castle, the road flattened out and straightened and in no time we were entering Versailles.

We passed through a poorly planned area of small businesses that were not well maintained before we drove into the center of the very pretty little town. The town seemed vibrant, well taken care of, with a lot of activity. The people walking about looked purposeful. We turned left by an impressive courthouse, drove down a small incline, passing shops and restaurants, to a traffic light where we made a right turn onto Rose Hill Avenue. Historic Primrose Inn was located on Rose Hill Avenue five houses up from the traffic light on the right-hand side. It was a lovely street. Large older homes, well established, some nice landscaping, and all well maintained.

Historic Primrose Inn was set back from the road and stood majestically on its own large lot. It was gothic in appearance but not depressing, as had been Preston Hall. In fact, it fit in well with its neighbors and seemed to set the tone for the houses around it. All across the front was a handsome iron fence

"I would like to see inside," Doris announced, as I stopped the car on the road outside the inn and we looked at it over its front lawn.

"I'm not sure," I replied. "I certainly don't want to wait for a real estate person and would really like to do more research before I talk to anybody. I only added this place to our list because we were sort of passing by. It only marginally meets our criteria. Tell you what. After our stay in Columbus, why don't we head back to South Carolina this way, and I'll see in advance if we can stop and view it then?"

Doris wasn't too happy but agreed. "Okay. But drive around a little before we leave. I didn't know that this part of the world was so delightful. The stone walls remind me very much of the Cotswold's."

As we pulled away, I saw a man wearing a very strange looking outfit—a sort of jump suit and a hat with flaps coming down to cover the ears, but they were not tied into place; the flaps were flapping up and down as he walked. He was carrying an orange cone like the ones one sees on the highway where repairs are taking place. I thought no more about it at the time, but it did stay in my mind.

More beautiful scenery, then back onto the freeway system and off to Ohio.

"Do you want to give Geoffrey a call when we pass through Cincinnati?" I asked Doris, as we approached the merge of Interstate 75 and Interstate 71.

"We do need to tell them of our plans," Doris replied. "But let's wait until we get to Columbus."

Our oldest and the most thoughtful of our sons, Geoffrey, now lives in Cincinnati with his wife Emma. Emma is from Cincinnati and has a lot of family support there. They have two children, Ryan and Jack. Geoffrey is as practical as he is loving.

Our youngest son, Peter, is a sweet young man much like his older brother. He has moved for his job to a suburb just outside Cleveland. Peter is the sort of guy who always has a smile on his face, can turn his hand to anything, and is always willing to help. Both Doris and I adore Peter's wife, Emily. They have a good marriage. They have a little boy, Derick, and our precious girl baby grandchild, Chloe.

We're a close, but not a clingy family, and we have taken to calling our three sons "The Three 'C's'" because one is in Cincinnati, one is in Columbus, and one is in Cleveland. It's not original—there is even a highway that connects those three cities called the "Three C Highway." It is one of the silly sorts of things that Doris and I like to do. And even though we're not musical, sometimes Peter in Cleveland is "High C," Alec in Columbus is "Middle C," and Geoffrey is "Lower C." The boys don't really get it, but they don't seem to mind.

The one that we worry about our middle son, and Middle C, Alec is one of the most loving and caring individuals that one could wish to meet, but he has yet to grow into maturity. He will get the craziest harebrained schemes into his mind and attack them with a vengeance. One never knows what he is going to come up with next. It is also seemingly impossible for him sit down quietly even for a second; he fidgets and talks incessantly.

We worry about his wife as well. Both are nurses at The Ohio State University, and Mary has ambition to go on and obtain an advanced degree. Alec has the ambition to be the best singer at karaoke night clubs and various bars up and down High Street, which runs through The Ohio State University campus in Columbus. Both Doris and I feel that the marriage won't last and are happy that there are no children involved. We don't want either of them to be hurt too much, but some pain will be inevitable. We merely hope to stay close and be a resource when the eventual split occurs. By the way

Mary is quiet and thoughtful—the very antithesis of our middle son. Alec has yet to grow into adulthood. Doris and I are not sure that Mary is the best match for Alec, or he for her. We have noticed that, increasingly, while Alec is ranting on about his latest scheme or idea, Mary moves into another world and appears not to listen.

"It's quiet time, Alec," she'll murmur, almost under her breath. He usually doesn't pay even the slightest attention. We are very fond of Mary and hope that she will still be there when Alec finds his way back to Mother Earth.

"Why did she marry him?" Doris says to nobody in particular, after each time we see them.

We were staying with Alec and Mary during this visit in part to gain more insight into their current relationship. We also had many friends in the area remaining from the time when this had been our home.

It was late when we arrived, and we were pleasantly surprised to find them both at home. Mary had prepared a light supper, and Alec wanted to mix drinks. At first, we talked about this and that—"How are you?" "What's new?"—but we didn't mention our plans until after the meal. We thought that perhaps there was hope for a discussion, but our middle son was soon bouncing off the walls and getting worked up over nothing. We looked at Mary with understanding, but she returned our look with sadness in her eyes. It was time to tell them our plans.

"We are leaving South Carolina," I announced. "We can't afford green greens and don't want to be a part of it any longer."

"What will you do?" Mary asked.

"Well. We're thinking of running a bed and breakfast."

"A bed and breakfast," Alec said. "That's awesome. Can I come and help be a part of it? I can fry eggs. I can butter toast. I can vacuum rooms. I can help little old ladies with the luggage. I can—"

"Hold on, Alec," I interrupted. "We have to find a suitable bed and breakfast first, and you have responsibilities here to take care of."

"Can I help you look?"

"Alec." This was from his mother. "We are not quite yet in our dotage. We'll find the right place, and then you can come and visit."

That quieted him down.

"We also haven't told your brothers, and I want them to hear it from us," I interjected. "So no letting the cat out of the bag."

"Where are you looking?" asked Mary.

"Mostly in the south," I said. "Away from the cold, if possible."

"Awesome," Alec said.

"Can I use your computer while I'm here?" I asked.

"Of course," Mary said. "Anytime, anything that you want."

"Well, we've had a long day," I said. "Thanks for everything. We'll be off to bed and will catch up some more tomorrow."

"Awesome."

"Later dude." This was Doris just as we retired to our bedroom.

"He hasn't changed much, has he?" Doris said, as we were getting undressed for bed.

I shook my head. "I'm afraid not," I said. "I love him to death but can't imagine how Mary puts up with him."

"What a worry. What went wrong?" Doris asked.

"Who knows, but we have to take care of our own problems first, and basically their situation is none of our business. Try and think about the bed and breakfasts that we've seen and maybe in the morning we'll know if any of them so far is the one we want to bid on."

"Goodnight, Derick."

"Goodnight, Doris."

The next morning, I woke thinking that maybe Historic Primrose Inn in Versailles, Kentucky should be a higher candidate on my list. The Kentucky scenery was very appealing, and the inn stood tall and proud in a pretty little town.

Alec and Mary had both left for work but left a note indicating that I could use their computer, so I got online and tried to find out as much as I possibly could about the Historic Primrose Inn. There was actually a lot of information all over the Internet, and I was quite proud of myself as I put together a profile for Doris.

"It does push our envelope to the edge," I told her. "It is probably within our range but only just."

"What does that mean?" Doris asked.

"Well, it means that if we can get financing, it will be at our outer limit. The inn will have to do well to pay for itself. It also means that some of the more conservative banks won't touch us; we'll have to go after the more creative ones out there."

"How do we do that?"

"We use a broker, someone who will play one bank or lending institution off against another to get the best deal for us."

"Do you know a broker?"

"No, but I'll bet that the karaoke kid, in whose house we're staying, knows several. These guys are just like Middle C—live life to the fullest and move in the same circles."

"Awesome."

"Oh, cut it out, Doris."

"I just want to see inside of the inn before I make my decision."

"Me, too, Miss awesome. I'll try and set that up for us."

I called Historic Primrose Inn and spoke to a very helpful woman. I was surprised to learn that the inn was not listed with a broker but was for sale by the owner. I asked if we could stop by and talk to them and was told "yes." I made an appointment for us and told Doris that we would have to tell the other boys sooner rather than later about our decision because Alec could only keep a secret for twenty-four hours, at most. She agreed and was happy that we were going back to Versailles.

The next day we drove to Cleveland to see Peter and the family there. All was well—happy just like peas in a pod. We shared our news, and they were enthusiastic for us, promising any and all help needed. We told them that because we had this new plan for the bed and breakfast thing, this coming Christmas would probably be our last Christmas in South Carolina. If they wanted to come on down for one more time, they were more than welcome. They said that they would look into it.

We stopped off in Columbus again on our way back south and asked Alec if he knew of any mortgage brokers. Of course, Alec knew just the guy to help us find the best financing, or so he said. I thanked him, avoiding the word "awesome" in my response. I told him I would call as the prospect developed.

We drove on to Cincinnati but decided against spending the night with Geoffrey and Emma because there was so much going on with the children. However, we did spend an evening with them, and they too were brought up to date with our plans. Maybe they weren't as enthusiastic as the others about what we had in mind, but they didn't offer up any major road blocks either.

After that, another Marriott Courtyard—perhaps I was getting my status back up to expect freebees, and it struck me the wide differences between staying in a chain hotel and staying in a bed and breakfast. There were certain expectations in the hotels, the rooms were basically the same shape, the bathrooms had the towels and soap in the same places—there was nothing personal apart from a smiling reception clerk. In bed and breakfasts, at least in the ones that we had been looking at lately, nothing was standard, each was an entity unto itself, and each differed from each other enormously. Plus the people who ran them ranged from friendly but retiring to maniacs on the lunatic fringe. What is this new world that we were getting into?

CHAPTER 5

Finding Primrose Inn

The drive down through Kentucky the next day was uneventful. The weather was cold and grey, not the greatest of days for us to see Historic Primrose Inn in its best light. Flo took us off the Interstate at Georgetown and through the back roads to Versailles. More utterly beautiful scenery, more painted fences, and more stone walls.

"It does remind me of home," Doris noted. "Even the weather feels like England today."

We passed through a delightful little town called Midway, then continued on to Versailles.

Our appointment was for 10:30 AM to allow them time to clear up a little after breakfast, and I have learned my lesson with these innkeepers in that they don't like it if you show up early. I planned to arrive spot on time. Parking was to the right side of the house, and there was a semi-circular pathway leading to the front door. The parking lot was empty when we arrived.

I didn't know whether I should ring the bell or walk straight in and opted for ringing the bell.

A very unusual looking man greeted us. He must have been no more than five feet tall and was quite rotund. His large face, underneath a partially balding head, was round and smiley. I thought that he looked a little like a caricature of Red Skelton.

"The Andersons?" he asked.

"Yes," I said. "Derick and Doris."

"Do come in," he said, emphasizing the "do."

"I'm Miles." He extended his hand. "I'm part of the innkeeping team around here."

I was a little concerned and somewhat bothered by what seemed to me to be a very poorly executed British accent. I looked at Doris, who raised her eyebrows back at me. Neither Doris nor I have lost our British twang over the years, although we certainly use American words and expressions. So why was this man trying to sound like a Brit? He must know that a true Brit can tell a false British accent most of the time, and his was appalling.

"Before we delve further," he said, "I am obliged to inform you that we already have an offer from another party to buy the inn."

"Oh," was my reaction.

"No, no, no, no, no, dear chap, no, no," he went on. "The other offer is contingent on that party selling their property and securing adequate financing to purchase this property. To this point, that has not been achieved."

The accent was getting thicker, and I found it most disconcerting.

"Doris, do you want to carry on with this?"

Maybe I was hoping that Doris would say "no" so that I could get away from this guy. But Doris, trooper that she is, said, "As we are here and have gone to some trouble to get here, why don't we at least look around and find out a little about the business?"

"Excellent!" said Miles. "Let me get Catherine." And with that he took off toward the back of the house. Not only did he talk strangely, he also moved strangely—half running and half hopping with a little skip thrown in from time to time.

"Feel glad that he didn't say 'awesome,'" Doris whispered.

We had been left in a large entry hall with tall ceilings and Victorian furniture. To our right was a parlor decorated in the same Victorian manner and to our left was a library with what looked like more modern furniture. Ahead of us was a magnificent u-shaped staircase leading up to the next floor. Halfway up the stairs where it turned was a truly incredibly beautiful stained glass window that glowed with a warm yellow light as it caught the sunshine.

"Isn't that window something?" I mentioned to Doris.

"Yes it is," Doris replied. "I love it."

In no time Miles was back, half running and half hopping through the furniture, now with a woman in tow.

"Allow me to introduce Catherine." Miles almost bowed as he spoke.

"How do you do, Catherine? I'm Derick Anderson, and this is my wife Doris." I put my hand on Doris's upper arm as I spoke.

"Hello, I'm pleased to meet you," Catherine said, and thank goodness there was no fake accent—just a warm, sweet American voice. "Welcome to Primrose Inn."

"*Historic* Primrose Inn," Miles interjected.

Catherine smiled. "Welcome to *Historic* Primrose Inn."

Catherine was of normal height, so therefore she towered over Miles. She might have been a little overweight, but she carried it well. She smiled and had a wry look on her face; I thought that I was going to like Catherine.

"Miles has no doubt told you that we have an offer on the table to buy *Historic* Primrose Inn. But the offer has been on the table for more than six months now; I don't think it unethical to talk to other interested parties."

"Okay, and obviously we don't want to cause trouble, but as we're here it does seem to be a waste if we don't look around," I said.

"No, of course you should look around," Catherine said. "I'll tell you a little about of the history as we go. The house was built in 1823; it was built as a plantation house. Kentucky was a slave-owing state before the civil war. The walls are solid brick—they actually made the bricks on-site as they were building the house." Catherine gave a wall a hug as we passed through the doorway from the hall into the parlor.

"The basement is like the dry stone walls that one sees between the fields around here, and they were built by Irish immigrants," she said, as we moved on into the dining room.

"The ceilings are fourteen feet tall, and the floor is the original ash." Catherine was good and knew her stuff.

"We have seven guest rooms: one downstairs in the main house, just off the hall. Three are upstairs in the main house, two are over the garage, and the seventh room is a separate building that we now call 'The Cottage.' Originally, that building was the kitchen for the house and probably the place where the slaves slept. I'll show you around. We have come through the parlor."

It was cluttered with far too much furniture for our taste but probably in keeping with the Victorian theme.

The dining room where we were now standing was set up with individual tables, and on past a dutch door was a well-stocked butler's pantry that in turn led into a large, well-equipped kitchen.

"We have this large island in the kitchen that is a great help with food preparation and plating," she said.

From the kitchen, we could see out to the back yard where The Cottage stood, and beyond this was what appeared to be a horse barn.

"We have three acres here," Catherine said. "About one acre in the front, which includes the house, and two acres in the back. You can see the barn and the paddock out back."

"Any animals?" I asked.

"Not anymore. There are five stalls in the barn. If you wanted to keep a horse or two out there I think that you could."

We retraced our footsteps back through the dining room and parlor into the hall.

"This is the library," Catherine said, as she showed us into the other front room off the center hall. "We use it as an office."

From there, we went further down the hall and looked into the first guest room. The bed had not been made up from the night before. It was a large room that had a king size canopied bed in it. The furnishings were antique, or at least had an antique look to them.

"All our rooms have their own bathrooms," Catherine explained. "We use this ground floor guest room for some of our older guests or others who don't want to climb the stairs."

From the hall, we entered what was described as The Garden Room. This room was next to the kitchen in the back of the house. "This used to be an outside patio, but it has been enclosed to make it into an all season room with an outdoor feel." Another view of the back garden; it really was quite large.

"Let me show you upstairs." Catherine led us back into the center hallway. "Miles, you don't have to join us; just make yourself available for questions."

Miles hopped off back to the kitchen, and we climbed the impressive staircase.

"The stained glass window was made for the house by special order in Germany," Catherine told us. 'It faces north, so it catches all the light available all day."

At the top of the stairway, we stepped into a small hall which had two doors off on the left, one door and opening off on its right.

"Each of the two doors on the left lead into two small guest rooms, and the door on the right leads to our largest guest room." Catherine opened the door to each one. The small rooms had queen size beds, and the large room had a king size. Again, each room has its own individual bathroom.

We were impressed. The rooms were delightfully decorated and looked welcoming.

Through an opening, we could see a small doorway that revealed a washing machine and dryer, along with a line of shelves all loaded with bed linens and towels.

"This is our upstairs work station," Catherine said.

Back down the stairs and out through the main double doorway, we now walked the reverse way around the pathway that we had taken from the parking lot. Just off the parking lot, we entered a doorway next to a garage.

"We have two rooms in this annex," Catherine said. "One is over the kitchen, and the other is over the garage. The room over the garage is more like a small suite in that it has a separate sitting room and bedroom. The other room is the room directly over the kitchen."

We were impressed. Good sized rooms, each with queen size beds and each with Jacuzzis. The Jacuzzi in the room over the kitchen was in the bedroom whereas the Jacuzzi in the room over the garage was in the bathroom. Both rooms were nicely furnished and looked inviting.

We came back down the annex stairs, turned left past the garage toward the back yard, and Catherine took us down a short walkway to the cottage. "The Cottage," she explained, "is our most popular room."

Once down there we could see why. There was a low sloping roof that extended over a small private patio. Inside was an adequately sized living room, a good-sized bedroom with a queen size bed, a small kitchen with eating area, and a large bathroom. This bathroom, too, was equipped with another Jacuzzi.

"You have a lot to see," said Catherine. "Why don't I leave for a short while so that you can talk?"

"Thank you," Doris said.

"I'll be in the main house if you have any questions." And with that, Catherine left us in The Cottage.

"Whew," I said. "There is lot to absorb here. What are you thinking?"

"I like it," Doris answered, "but I want more time to look deeper and to think."

"I know," I answered. "Anyway, it might all be moot; they have that other offer on the table."

"Do you think that they will let us look around by ourselves? Without them tagging along?"

"We can but ask."

"I'd like to."

We made our way back to the kitchen in the main house and were greeted by the smell of freshly brewed coffee. Catherine and Miles were sitting on stools around the center island.

"I've just made some fresh coffee; would you like a cup?" Catherine asked.

I said, "Yes please," but Doris declined.

"Tea—I bet that she would prefer tea," Miles said.

Oh no, I thought. *How can she be so nice and he be such an utter asshole?*

"No tea, thanks, Miles," I answered. "We wouldn't want you to have to jump in the harbor, then swim around to find where you threw it."

He looked puzzled at first, but then the light dawned.

"Oh good one, old chap. I'll have to remember that. However, I'm sure that my ancestors were with the Tories."

"Mine were peasants, Miles," I said. "They were probably standing on the dock when your ancestors left saying, 'Come back—it's flat.'"

"Whatever," Catherine said, interrupting. "Do you have any questions?"

"Where do you live?" Doris asked.

"How silly of me," Catherine said and led us back through to the butler's pantry, where this time we turned right into a small passage way that was lined with more shelves.

"This is the downstairs workstation," Catherine said. "If you go straight, there is another washing machine and dryer but here—" and there was a door on the right, which she opened, "—are our quarters."

We were led into a large room that had a big bed, some chests of drawers, and a small table with two chairs. There was a bathroom and a large walk-in closet off the main room.

"This is where we spend our time when we want to get away from the guests," Catherine explained.

I was disappointed and therefore surprised that Doris didn't seem concerned or even want to ask about this room. Instead, she looked at Catherine and said, "What we would really like to do is look around by ourselves, if that is all right with you."

"Of course you do, and of course you can." Catherine was very understanding. "We do have a small problem with our staff arriving soon, and they don't know that the inn is for sale. You don't mind telling them that you are here to check the place over to see if it will accommodate a wedding, do you? That is, if you happen to run into them."

"No, we don't have a problem saying that," Doris replied. She and Catherine were beginning to bond. "Do you often get people who just want to look the place over?"

"All the time," Catherine answered.

I had only finished half of my cup of coffee, but Doris pulled me away and we set about looking the place over.

"Derick," she said, "can you and Miles stop this business of seeing who can pee highest up the wall. Tea in the harbor—and the world being flat!"

"I'm sorry, but that phony accent just gets up my nose."

"Oh, just get on with it."

We went everywhere that we could over this old house. Some of the rooms had not been made up from the night before while others had not been slept in. We actually said very little, but I could tell by the way that Doris was checking everything and every place that she could that she had interest—much more than any of our previous stops.

"I want you to find out what it will take to buy this place," she announced.

"You mean that I have to talk to that little pip squeak?" I said.

"Yes, and be nice. I'll be there to help you. Anyway, I have the feeling that Catherine is the one who makes the decisions, so we need to include her also."

"Oh-tay." I did my Buckwheat impression. "Lead me into battle."

Catherine and Miles were in the parlor this time, and that is where we joined them. Outside, I noticed the man dressed in a jumpsuit and wearing a hat with untied flaps carrying a bright orange roadway cone. I remembered that I'd seen exactly the same sight when we were here before on our drive-by.

"It's Grayson George," Catherine explained. "He's our handyman. He's on his way to clean the fish pond."

"Why the orange cones?" I asked.

"Oh, he has several," Miles said. "The man is crazy. He sets the cones out wherever he is working because he worries that a guest might trip over a wire or slip on a slick spot and then sue him. He also carries a rubber hammer with him wherever he goes. God knows why."

"He works for you?" I asked.

"Not me!" Miles said, nearly shivering. "He works for Catherine."

"Grayson has been at the inn longer than you, Miles," Catherine interjected, "and he is a wonderful asset."

I was confused but let it go, as we had many other things to discuss.

"The asking price for the inn is one million two hundred and fifty thousand," I stated.

"Yes," Catherine said. "But feel free to make an offer."

"What comes with that?"

"Well, we are selling the inn turnkey," Catherine said. "That means that with a few exceptions, and we have a list, you get everything that you see, including whatever is in the refrigerator. That way you can just walk in and continue the business."

"We also offer training," Miles added. "We'll stay on for two weeks after the sale to show you the ropes."

"Why are you selling?" I looked directly at Catherine.

"We've been here long enough," she said. "We own some land in Florida, along with other family members, and we want to move down there, build a house that we might turn into a part-time bed and breakfast. But mainly we want to be with family on a private family compound."

"What is your occupancy rate?" I asked, trying to sound like I knew what I was talking about.

"That would be 62 percent."

"What about the Average Daily Rate?"

"One hundred thirty-eight dollars."

Even though I was new to all of this, both of those numbers sounded good to me. The inn was doing a lot of business but still had room for growth, and the money coming in was good enough that we would not have to increase the prices right away.

"Are you busy year round?" Doris asked.

"Not really," Catherine replied. "We are always full for Keeneland racing both in the spring and in the fall. Keeneland is our local thoroughbred racing track just down the road. We are so-so busy during most of the summer, but business usually falls off during the winter months. That's when we try and get away. We have names of inn sitters who we have used in the past if you want to do the same."

"Inn sitters?" I enquired.

"Yes, people who move in when you are not here and run the inn. Of course they take all your profits, but at least it gives you a chance to get away."

"What about the other offer on the table?" I was looking at Catherine.

"It's a younger couple; they are currently in Detroit and not enjoying life there. They want to move south and have aspirations of running a bed and breakfast. They like the inn and have made an offer. Their offer has contingencies. One is that they have to sell their house in Detroit, and the second is that they have to secure adequate financing for their purchase of the inn. There doesn't appear to be any problem with them getting financing as long as they get a good price for the house that they have for sale. But they're having trouble selling the Detroit house."

Doris joined into the conversation. "I feel sorry for them."

"So do I," said Catherine. "But I'm beginning to feel sorry for us, too. It has been more than six months since we accepted their offer."

"Is there a time limit?" I asked.

"There is an escape clause," Catherine said, nodding. "We can accept another offer and tell them that we intend to accept it. They then have seven days to make good on their offer, and if they can't, we are free to accept the new one."

"So if we were to make a bid," I said, "you tell them and they have seven days to finalize their bid. If they can't come through, we bump them?"

It was Miles's turn. "Right," he said. "But we have to accept your counter bid, and that would have to be close to what has been already offered by the original party."

"Do you understand?" Catherine asked. "Your offer has to be close enough to theirs for us to accept it."

"Will you tell us what their offer is?" I asked.

"No," Miles said, and I realized that he had just peed higher up the wall than me.

There was a period of silence before I said to Doris, "Our schedule is way off now. We have been here much longer than anticipated, and we ought to be making tracks. Do you have any more questions for Catherine and Miles?"

"I know that as soon as we leave, I'll have a million more things that I'll want to ask, but I know that we need to be on the road."

Catherine nodded. "You can call at any time or email. If you should bump into Grayson on the way out, remember that he is not to know that you are here as prospective buyers, although he is pretty intuitive and probably has an idea what is going on."

"No problem," Doris said. "And thank you for everything."

We headed for the door, and Miles showed us out. I think that he said goodbye but couldn't be certain.

As luck would have it, Grayson must have finished his fish pond duties and was now attaching some Christmas lights around the trunk of a large oak tree near the parking area where our car was. Several cones were placed around where he was working, and the rubber hammer lay on the ground next to them.

It would have been rude not to acknowledge him as we passed, so I nodded and said a quick "hello."

He nodded back, but I could tell he was really checking us out.

"Getting ready for Christmas?" I asked.

Another nod but no words of reply.

"Catherine says that you are invaluable around here," Doris added.

SEMI-RETIREMENT

More nods and maybe a smile.

"I maintain the place," Grayson said at last. "The house and the gardens. I have a degree in horticulture."

"You do?" I got into the conversation. "Then perhaps you can tell me. Why do they call the grass that grows around here, bluegrass?"

Grayson looked puzzled. "Hmm...." Then he added, "What to say! What to say! What to say." Then, "Hmm...." again, and finally, "I don't know!"

This wasn't getting anywhere, so we both went back to nodding at each other while Doris and I made steps toward our car. We got in and started up, but before I put the gear lever into reverse, I noticed another vehicle making its way up the driveway. This newly arrived vehicle gave a whole new and different meaning to the word "hybrid" car. This vehicle seemed to be comprised of several cars, or parts from several cars, that had been cobbled together to make one new car. Nothing matched—some panels were one color and other panels a quite different color. Windows were missing, and in some places, cardboard was stuffed into open spaces. The car was filthy dirty. The noise it made was spectacular, as was the smoke and steam mainly but not restricted to emitting from the rear end. It pulled into an empty parking space, and the engine must have been turned off because the fury of the exiting smoke subsided, but the car didn't stop moving. It shuddered and shook and shuddered and shook and shuddered again and again. Nobody got out.

"Let's go, Derick," Doris commanded. "It's nothing to do with us."

"But I want to know—" I protested.

Doris interrupted. "No, you don't need to know anything. Let's be on our way."

I reversed our car, put the gear lever into drive, and we headed back down the driveway. We turned left out of the drive, back through town, back to the freeway, on to a long journey back to South Carolina.

We had covered quite a few miles before either of us spoke. It was me who broke the silence.

"What do you think?"

"I liked it."

"What about the owner's quarters? It's just a bedroom."

"I know, but you can block the whole back end of the house off, and we could use the Garden Room as a sitting area for us."

"What about the décor?"

"Not good. Victorian has never been one of our choices. But everything that we saw was cluttered. I'm thinking that if we cleaned out some of the excess, we would finish up with something that we could live with."

"Remember that they are selling the place turnkey, so they're not thinking of taking anything much with them. This will mean that we would be presented with a problem of incorporating our stuff in with what is already there, and nothing that we have is Victorian."

"Even more reason to throw the bad crap out." Doris's mind must have really been working away.

"What about the location?"

"Perfect. It's away from the coast, close to the three C's, and in some of the most beautiful countryside that I've seen, reminding me of England."

"That's because it looks a lot like England, but it could be far enough north that there will be snow, and we wanted to stay away from snow if we could."

"Well, there won't be as much snow as in Ohio, and it won't be as hot as South Carolina. I think that we can live with it."

"What about the price?"

"Oh, that's your problem."

"My problem!" I protested. "Why is it *my* problem?"

"Well, you are going to have to figure out how to get along a little better with Miles."

"How can I do that?" I was hurt. "How can anybody take seriously a little pip squeak who looks like a cut down version of Red Skelton and is trying to sound like Noel Coward?"

"As I said, you're going to have to find a way of getting along a little better with Miles."

"But it is a lot more than that, Dolly," I said. "First of all, we have to sell our house. Then we have to secure financing to buy the inn. Then we have to put in an offer that meets or betters what they have on the table. Then we have to wait seven days for the other party to either withdraw or better our offer."

"And we have to make nice to Miles, so that he helps us and doesn't get in the way," she added.

"Are you absolutely sure that this is the inn that we should buy?" I asked.

"It's the best that you've shown me so far. If you like it, go for it. Don't let the grass grow under your feet even if the grass is not tolerant to salt in the water."

I thought ahead to what seemed like a nightmare but had to admit that this was the best that we had seen. Nothing comes without an effort, but dear Lord, where does one start?

I was lucky in that Doris fell off to sleep for most of the drive back south, and this gave me time to think and then arrange those thoughts into a plan of action. The first thing was to contact the real estate office at the club and talk to them about listing the South Carolina house at a price where it would sell pretty quickly. Then I would have to write a business plan—one that the bankers would need to see when I asked them for a mortgage on the inn. Then I needed to contact Alec and ask him for names of mortgage brokers so that I could get approval for the financing. Then I needed to puzzle out an appropriate bid for the inn. My guess is that the offer they already had on the table was pretty close to the asking price, but that was only a guess. Perhaps I could get some advice along those lines. I would probably also need to hire an independent appraiser, and where was I going to find one of those? Such a lot to do.

CHAPTER 6

Sell a House, Buy an Inn

I'm not sure if I was hearing good news because I wanted to hear good news or if it *really was* good. The real estate office at the Club said that they maintained a list of prospective buyers interested in buying property on the island. As long as we didn't ask for more than was reasonable, we would probably sell our house in a very short period of time.

Alec said that he knew just the right person to act as a mortgage broker. His name was Henry, and Henry told me that I didn't need a business plan and that he could get us fixed with a good mortgage as long as we obtained a good appraisal on the inn. He went on to explain that if we were prepared to pay $4,000 for an appraisal instead of the usual local $300/$400, he knew just the place to get a good appraisal carried out. "The better the appraisal, the better the rate," he told us. "You'll save the cost of the appraisal in the first two months of mortgage payments." We told him to go ahead and set it up.

Christmas was getting nearer, and the whole family was still planning on coming down, so with those two pieces of good news, Doris and I could devote more time to decorating the South Carolina house for the holiday and planning. We did want to look at Historic Primrose Inn at least one more time before we made an offer, and we decided that we would try and arrange this for early in the New Year.

The family all arrived tired after their travels but happy to be together. Our Christmas holiday was spectacular—the best that we have ever spent. It was a mild Christmas weather-wise in South Carolina that year, and we got a permit from the club to build a bonfire on the beach. The boys dug a hole in the sand and collected driftwood for the fire. The rest of us prepared food. In addition to the bonfire, we took a small hibachi grill to fix small steaks, hamburgers, and hot dogs. It was a wonderful evening. We ran races along the surf line, improvised a soccer game, and sat huddled around our fire while we grilled our food and gorged ourselves. The memory of that evening will stay with Doris and me forever.

The next day, Christmas Day, provided more good memories as the house filled with laughter and shouts of delight over Christmas gifts. As the day progressed and the children settled down to play with their new toys, the aroma of a turkey being cooked wafted out of the kitchen. I asked the three boys if we could have a family conference about our new endeavor.

Generally, they were all supportive. Alec was overly supportive. They all said that they wanted to come to Kentucky as soon as they could if we were successful in buying the inn. They all said they would help us with the move if needed. Alec wanted to take over the negotiations, planning, and arrangements, but his brothers talked him out of it, reminding him that he had his own life to live and to let his parents run theirs the way that his parents saw fit.

"I am a little concerned," I confided to Doris later. "This is all going so well that something has to go astray sometime because that's just the way of things."

"You'll handle it," she said.

We made an appointment to stop by the inn for another look around the place in early January. Doris had wanted to wait a little longer, but I was concerned about the other offer and had just about convinced myself that Miles had contacted the other party and told them about us. Doris didn't agree with that but did agree to an early January visit. I asked her if she wanted me to find additional properties to look at when we made the trip and she said, "No, let's win or lose this one first before we go off in another direction."

We heard from Henry that he had contacted the perfect appraisal company who would look over not just the inn but the books as well. It was going to cost us $4,800. I said okay and told him to go ahead with those arrangements.

Once again, the car was loaded and once more, we set off north. This time we were spending the night in Historic Primrose Inn, and I must say we were looking forward to it.

The journey was long, but we had made an early start so it was early afternoon when we pulled into the Historic Primrose Inn parking lot. Miles and Catherine were there to greet us and for that night, they put us up in the suite over the garage.

"We wanted to put you into The Cottage," Catherine said, "but it has been booked. However, you can be quiet in the attic suite. I'm sure that you have a lot to talk about." Miles was actually pleasant and helped with our bags.

"Do you think that Catherine has had words with him?" I asked Doris.

Doris merely raised her eyebrows.

"Your appraiser was here," Miles informed us. "Nice young man, very interested in old houses. He actually got confused and lost on one of the back staircases, but I was there to come to the rescue."

Throughout the rest of the afternoon and into the early evening, we went over and through every inch of the inn, or as much of it as we could. I went into the attics—there were two—and into the basements; there were two of them also.

Miles was still much less aggressive than at our previous visit, and I became convinced that he had been given a talking to in the same way that I had.

Catherine and Miles showed us everything: how they made reservations, how they kept their books, the maintenance records, storage areas, cleaning equipment—everything. Miles showed us all of the mechanics, and while explaining how to operate the generator that they had on standby in case of a loss of power, Doris and Catherine went off to the parlor with a bottle of wine and two glasses. It was a very full and rewarding day.

I asked Catherine for a recommendation for dinner on our first night, and she informed us that a new restaurant had just opened down the hill and around the corner.

"It's called Mandy's," Catherine said. "Small, casual, and a little on the country side but close enough for you to walk there and back."

This suited us just fine, and as the town hall clock was striking eight, another memory from our life in England, we made our way down Rose Hill Avenue absorbing the ambiance of this sweet little town and beginning to feel at home.

Mandy's was still quite busy. Doris and I were shown to a booth and asked if we wanted anything prior to our meal. I ordered martinis but was informed that they only served beer or wine.

"What wines do you have?" I asked, wanting to sound like an expert even though I was anything but.

"Red or White?"

"Two glasses of Red, please."

Our waitress was just a sweet young thing, and as it turned out, too young to serve wine according to Kentucky law. Our overly filled glasses were delivered to us by a much more mature woman, who set them in front of us with great aplomb.

"Two glasses of Merlot," she announced with a smile. "Are you new in town or just passing through?"

I don't know why—and halfway through my explanation I realized that Doris was getting upset with me—but I proceeded to tell this woman that we were in town as prospective buyers of the bed and breakfast up the hill.

"You are, are you?" she said. "I'm Elsie, Mandy's mother, and it looks like we may become neighbors. Welcome to Versailles."

"Well, we're not there, or here, yet," I said. "We're just in the looking phase right now."

"I can't wait to tell Mandy," Elsie said. "Don't rush off after your meal; I'm sure that she'll want to talk to you."

When she left, Doris looked daggers at me.

"Do you have to tell everybody our life story? She's a complete stranger."

"Sorry, Dolly. I got carried away."

"There are times, Derick, when you do need to be carried away—carried away in a straight jacket if you ask me. Anyway, let me tell you some news after my chat with Catherine this afternoon. Catherine and Miles are not married. In fact, Miles has nothing more to do with the inn than helping Catherine get through the day. Maybe he helps her get through the night, too, but we didn't go to that depth in our first conversation."

Women do have a way of finding out what is important, I thought, impressed. Doris went on.

"It seems that Catherine's husband and the father of her children was known to drink, and he killed himself in an automobile accident five years ago. The children, there are two of them, are grown and had moved away before the accident, so Catherine was left by herself. She found Miles at a cooking exhibition at the Kentucky State Fair in Louisville. He was just sitting next to her and they started talking. At the time, she thought he was visiting from England and was lost. She wanted to help him."

"Poor woman," I said, shaking my head.

"He's not English, of course, but his parents screwed him up by telling him that they are distantly related to the Queen. They told him, and who knows why? that way back in the day, long before the present Queen ascended to the thrown, there was a falling out in the royal family and some of family members secretly emigrated to the United States while the other side of the family stayed in England and eventually went on to rule the country. Miles was a descendent of the part of the family who came to America. All of this was hushed up at the time for political reasons, but the British authorities know it. His parents went on tell him that under certain circumstances the American side of the family—Miles' especially while he was alive could be called on to reclaim the crown and return to rule England. Miles has been spending his whole life getting ready for his ascendancy to the throne, when all this will be revealed."

"Good God." I didn't know what else to say.

"When he was a teenager, they took him for speech therapy because they thought that there was something wrong with his voice. The therapist told them that there was nothing wrong with his voice and that Miles was just working on perfecting an English accent in case there was ever a need. But Miles didn't tell the therapist what the need might be."

"King Miles doesn't have a very authentic ring," I said.

"Stop it, Derick, and don't you dare let on that I've told you any of this."

"The whole thing sounds unbelievable. Some people are incredibly naïve. What do you think? Miles helps Catherine during the night as well as the day?"

"Now stop, Derick, don't be inappropriate. Thank goodness our food looks as if it is coming."

The meal was more than delicious, it was spectacular, and not spoilt one little bit by the coarse red wine. The portion sizes were enormous, and we should have just ordered one dessert between us and that would have been enough.

Feeling full and relaxed, I asked for the check. It came, and I used my credit card to pay. Our sweet young waitress came back with our receipt and asked us not to leave because Mandy and her mother wanted to talk to us. We didn't have to wait for long before Mandy and Elsie worked their way through the tables with two more glasses of the coarse red wine.

Mandy was a delight—short, bleached blonde hair, broad smile, and a twinkle in her eye.

"I hear that you are going to buy Primrose Inn?" she said.

"Not yet." I told her that we were only here to look, and we hadn't made an offer yet.

"Well, it's not that I'm a busy body or even a nosy neighbor, and I've been thinking whether I should say this or not, but I don't like the man, so I want to warn you about Miles." Mandy went on. "He's not to be trusted."

I was getting too much information for one day, and my mind was tilting into overload. "Well…. Thanks for the warning, but I don't know what to say."

"He's going around town telling everybody that he has sold the inn and that they are moving to Florida in maybe just a few weeks. You should look over the deed closely because the inn is not his to sell."

"Mandy, I know that you are only trying to help, but we haven't made an offer yet."

"He says that you have."

"There is another couple interested in the inn."

Mandy didn't want to give up.

"We all love Catherine," she added. "And we all loved David, her husband. It was so sad when he died. Nobody trusts Miles. That's all, and we think that you should know."

Elsie stood there next to Mandy with a stern look on her face, and then she added her own two cents on the matter. "Mandy is right. She wasn't going to mention it, but I told her that she must. He's no good, that Miles. Just a lousy waste of space if you ask me."

"Well…." I was back to saying "Well" a lot, probably because I was confused and hadn't asked anybody for their opinions. "Well…that's nice of you to share your thoughts with us, and we will be sure to look everything over in the greatest of detail if we ever get that far."

"Enjoy the wine."

They nodded, and as Elsie was leaving, she turned and said, "If you do buy the inn and need some help, keep me in mind."

Help doing what? I thought. "Thanks, Elsie. We have to be going now, don't we, Doris."

"Yes," Doris replied. She had been no help whatsoever during this exchange, and I wanted to tell her that.

We left and headed back up the hill to the inn.

"Thanks for your help back there," I said.

"Oh, I was speechless," she replied. "I've heard about small towns where everybody knows everybody's business, but how can they know, or think that they know, about us before we even get here?"

"Beats me."

Doris wasn't finished. "It's funny though, much as I don't understand, I sort of like Mandy and her mother, and I think that they were not being nosey. They really were looking to help us."

"I hope so," I replied, "because if we do move here, I intend to be a regular at Mandy's restaurant. The food was spectacular."

We were fortunate that our room for the night had its own separate entrance at the side of the house, so we didn't have to talk to anybody when we got back to the inn. We simply climbed some stairs, turned left, closed our door, and locked it.

"It's been a funny day," I mumbled. We were both obviously tired out.

Doris just shook her head but then said, "It has been odd, but you know, I'd rather be doing this than watching grass die."

"Me, too, Dolly. Good night."

We slept incredibly well; it was quiet, and the bed was very comfortable. We appreciated the oversized bathroom and the quality of soaps and toiletries provided. We woke refreshed without the alarm, took showers, then went down to breakfast.

To get to the dining room, we had to go outside and walk around the front of the house. However, even though it was January, the weather wasn't too bad at all. *Good old Kentucky*, I thought to myself, as I remembered other Januarys in Ohio.

Once inside the front door, we were struck by the aromas of breakfast coming from the kitchen.

Miles was there hopping around tables topping up juice glasses and coffee cups.

"Do come in," he called to us. "Here, I've set you up on the table nearest to the kitchen."

The room was barely half-full of people—only another two tables were in use. A third table looked as if somebody had been there earlier and left.

"Tea is it, then, with your breakfast?" Miles asked.

"No, coffee," I said. "We prefer coffee, thank you." I wanted to make some remark about him not having the ability to make a proper cup of tea, but I was on my best behavior and determined not to be the cause of any rift.

"Coffee it is then? How about juice?"

"Orange juice would be nice, thank you. Doris, would you care for any juice?"

"No thank you," she answered.

Miles poured juice into the glass that had been set out in front of Doris and left the glass in front of me empty. I thought that he had just made a mistake, so I stretched out to reverse the glasses. He was hovering around the table and when he saw what I was doing, he went off again with his little Noel Coward impersonation.

"Dear boy, dear boy, dear boy. No, no, no. Don't stretch across the table if the glass has been filled incorrectly. One must simply get up and exchange seats."

I looked at Doris for help. If this was going to be the tone of the day, I would end up by decking the guy. Doris must have guessed how I was feeling, so she simply picked up her glass with the orange juice and handed it to me. "Yours, I believe," she said.

"All part of the training." Miles was back into his Noel Coward. "You have to make the guests like you and by acting silly every now and then, you'll have them rolling their eyes and laughing like loons."

"I shot a loon once, Miles," I told him. "We were on vacation in Canada. I might have broken the law, but I had to quiet the wretched bird and shooting it was the only way."

Miles just stared at me in response, then disappeared by hopping back into the kitchen.

Doris stared me down. "Derick, you've never shot a loon. You don't even have a gun—you hate guns."

"I know, but I shut the little pip squeak up for a few minutes, didn't I?" I said, smiling.

"Please, Derick, be nice to him. Just for a little while, just do it for me."

Catherine popped her head out of the kitchen and said, "Good morning! I'm a little busy but will come out when I can."

"No problem, Catherine," Doris answered.

"I do like that woman," Doris said, when Catherine had gone back into the kitchen.

"So do I," I said.

Breakfast was served. Miles hopped from table to table as he brought out plates of bacon, eggs, and caramel French toast. The eggs were served in a small ramekin, and Miles described them as "Eggs Extravaganzas."

It was obvious that Miles enjoyed saying "Eggs Extravaganzas," because he repeated it often. Every time he put a plate down, out came, "Eggs Extravaganzas" with great flourish.

When it was our turn to be served, he went through the same routine. "The dish that made the inn famous—'Eggs Extravaganzas.'"

"You have to put on a show," he whispered to me. "It's not just the food alone."

I was lost, but I was good this time and didn't say anything. I wanted to point out that there were three things on the plate and just because the names of the other two—bacon and French toast—don't have the same pizzas as eggs extravaganzas shouldn't mean that they didn't need to be mentioned. Besides, most of the other guests were looking at each other with amazement and just a little embarrassment at his *show*. I was good and just smiled.

No matter how the breakfast was served, the food tasted really good and the coffee was strong and tasty also. Miles kept the coffee cups filled. He tried to engage others in conversation, but either they were confused by the phony British accent or had nothing much to say to him, and he didn't get very far with most of his attempts.

As we were finishing our meal, Catherine came out of the kitchen still wearing her apron and a smile. She went around the other tables and made sure that everybody was happy with their meals and then sat down at our table with a cup of coffee.

"How was the room?" she asked. "Did you sleep well?"

"The room was fine, and we slept like tops," Doris answered.

"How about Mandy's?"

My turn to answer. "Interesting," I said. "Good food."

Catherine looked a little puzzled. "We haven't been able to eat there as much as we would like because she closes at 9:00 PM. Most of the time, we don't get a chance to eat until later than that. But I'm told that it is very good. Mandy has worked here at the inn in the past as a housekeeper. She has also helped out in the kitchen when we've needed it, so I know that she knows a thing or two about cooking. Mandy and her mother were great friends with my husband before he died."

Before we could reply, Miles stopped by the table. "How were the Eggs Extravaganzas?" he asked.

We said, "Fine." He left to go and talk to the paying guests.

After he left, Catherine fixed us with a stare and said, "I've told him many, many times that it is Eggs Extravaganza, singular, and not Eggs Extravaganzas, plural, but he won't get it. I just don't have the energy to go there again."

There was some exasperation in Catherine's tone, and at that moment, I felt a little sorry for her.

"Do you have to rush off, or would you like to look around some more?" Catherine asked. "Miles will be busy for a while checking people out. He loves to operate the credit card machine."

"We don't need to see anything else, and we have just a few questions about staff."

"'Technically, we don't have any staff," Catherine explained. "They are self-employed, and we hire them by the hour. There are two people who come on a regular basis, and I have a backup list of others if needed, which is not very often. Grayson is the handy man who can turn his hand to just about anything. He can be challenging at times, he doesn't get along too well with Miles, and in truth he didn't get along too well with my husband back then either. He's quite eccentric in a lot of ways, but he is honest and reliable. He can always be counted on to show up, or to work extra hours if we need him.

"Linda is our housekeeper, and she is quite different. Linda is a more mature woman who has never really matured. She is good-natured but completely financially irresponsible. We think that she is honest, but to her understanding of the word 'honest,' nobody else's. She looks a lot like rural Kentucky; if you ever meet her, you'll know what that means. I think that she has four grown children but never talks about them. Her husband, father of the children, left for somewhere out of state, south I believe, many years ago, and she never talks about him. There have been a series of 'other men'—the current one has been asked not to come here. He's...well, it's really none of my business." Catherine paused to take a sip of her coffee.

"We haven't told either Grayson or Linda of our plans to sell the inn," she added, "but they talk together and might have some idea. Grayson more so than Linda."

"Would they stay on if we asked them?" Doris asked.

"I'm not sure about Grayson, but Linda for sure. She is quite poor and needs the money. Grayson might stay on if you ask him properly. He doesn't have much in the bank either, but his needs, especially when it comes to beer and cigarettes, are a lot less than Linda's."

There was a pause before I said, "Thanks for all the help and information. We won't say anything to your staff. You ought to know that we are leaning toward making an offer. We still have some final bits and pieces to check out in our minds and different aspects to consider, so we'll see. However, let me ask you a question."

She nodded. "Okay."

"Do you think that we'll make good innkeepers?"

"That's tough to answer because I don't know you very well. You seem diligent in your research, which is a good thing and probably means that you care about the details. You do seem to have the capacity for hard work, which you'll need. You are amiable and will get along with folks; and even though I sense that you don't believe this, Miles is very good at getting along with folks. Other than that, it will be what you make it."

"Good." I turned to Doris. "Are you ready to hit the road? Or is there anything additional that you want to discuss?"

She shook her head. "No, I'm good to go. Shall we say good-bye to Miles?" Doris was a good woman and very thoughtful about details.

"And how much do we owe you for the night's stay and breakfast?" I added.

"Nothing," said Catherine. "Let's hope that something comes of all this. Miles," she called out, "The Andersons are leaving."

Miles hopped in from the kitchen where he had been washing dishes.

"What has gotten into you, Miles?" Catherine asked. "You never do the washing up."

"Just trying to show a good example," Miles said. "Do you have to go? Maybe stay for another cup of coffee?"

"No we have to go, we'll be in touch though," I said.

With that we were out of the door, maybe rushing a little faster than we otherwise would have—especially me. I didn't want Miles to start up another conversation.

"Catherine is so nice," I said to Doris, as we pulled out of the drive. "I think that she will help a lot if we buy this inn and can show us a lot."

"You're right, Derick, she is nice."

"One thing before we leave town: I think that we need a lawyer in Versailles to look after our interests."

Doris looked at me as if amazed at my forethought.

"How will you do that?" she asked.

"Well, I thought I'd ask Mandy if she has any suggestions. We'll just stop in as we pass."

Mandy's restaurant front door was locked and the sign said "Closed," but we could hear voices and clattering from inside. We went around to the back and saw that the back door was ajar. Mandy and her mother were in the kitchen preparing vegetables.

"Hello, Mandy," I called out.

She turned. "Oh hello," she said, as she recognized us.

"Mandy, I wanted to ask your advice. Is there a lawyer in town who you could recommend if we buy Primrose Inn?"

Without a moment's hesitation, she said, "James Macready. He has worked with us, and I highly recommend him. Are you thinking of buying the inn?"

"No, we're still debating, but we wanted our ducks in a row if do decide to move on it."

"I've got one of Jim's cards somewhere, let me look. By the way, I hope that you don't think that we were too forward last evening."

"No, not at all, Mandy," I said, even though I had. "We find Miles a little unusual also."

Doris joined in. "Derick told Miles at breakfast this morning that he was going to shoot him."

"I did no such thing!"

"Miles said that he was a bird, and you told him that you like to go around shooting birds, that's all."

"Miles said that he was a bird?" Mandy asked, handing over the card she'd found. She had a puzzled look on her face.

"You had to be there," I answered.

With so much to think about, there was not a lot of conversation between us on the drive back down south. I wanted to ask Doris if she was still keen on pursuing Primrose Inn, but

I didn't want to hear a negative answer. However, all this was made a lot easier after a cell phone call I received just east of Knoxville.

"Derick, this is Henry, the number one mortgage broker in the entire United States and the number one broker in your heart. And close friend of your favorite son, Alec."

"Hello, Henry. You sound chipper, but we don't favor any of our children over the others."

"Just got you approved, young man," he said.

I do hate being called a young man when I'm well into my sixties, especially by a kid who might be young enough to be my grandson.

"How can you do that when we haven't submitted an offer or established a price yet?" I asked.

"The appraisal. Remember I told you if we went in with a good appraisal everything would be okay?"

"Let me put you on speakerphone so that you can fill both of us in with the details." I pressed the speakerphone button. "Okay, you're on."

"Here it is then: I'll keep the numbers round for ease of understanding and because you are in your car. The house or rather the inn has appraised at $850,000 and the business at $250,000. The bank will loan you 80% of those at a rate of 8%. The current owners are asking $1,250,000 so offer them $1,000,000. If they accept, you need to put down $200,000 and the rest comes through the bank. At 8%, your monthly payments will be around $7,000. The inn brings in more than $20,000 on average each month, so you are ahead of the game. You're happy, the bank is happy, and by the way, I went through somebody that I know in Lexington and they are well aware of the potential of Versailles."

These numbers were so enormous to Doris and I that they just buzzed around in our heads for a while looking for a place large enough in our minds to accommodate them. They meant nothing to Henry; he was used to talking this way everyday, but Doris and I needed time for them absorb and maybe mature a little.

"We need to think about it, Henry, but thanks for your trouble here and for the quick turnaround. By the way, how do you get paid?"

"I take a half point at the closing," he replied. "You don't have to write a check or anything; it all gets taken care of in the paperwork."

Still reeling and with too much to consider, I said, "Thanks again. I'll call you tomorrow."

"Congratulations," he said. "You've got a good opportunity going here."

The phone disconnected.

"Why is he congratulating us?" Doris wanted to know. "And do you understand all those numbers?"

"I understand the principal, but I need a little time to get the small print into my head. I *think* that it's good news. We will realize more than $200,000 from the sale of our South Carolina home, but I don't think that Miles and Catherine will go down to $1,000,000. My guess is that their current offer is better than that."

"I agree. This is not going to be easy for you over the next few days. I know that you haven't asked me yet which way I'm leaning, but my gut is to go for it. I like both the inn and the location."

"We do need to contact that lawyer; I'll do that as soon as we get home." Then I added, "Can I have some quiet time for the rest of the journey just to think things out?"

"Of course."

By the time we arrived back home, I thought that I had a clear path in my mind. I would contact the club real estate office the next morning and list our house. I would phone Miles and ask him if $1,100,000 would be a realistic asking price.

Much as I didn't care for the pip squeak, I would just have to trust that he wouldn't use that information to force a decision out of the Detroit couple. I wanted to sleep on the plan overnight before doing anything. Doris was understanding to the extreme, and by the time that I had unloaded the car, she had a couple of cocktails ready.

"No more talk tonight," she said. "Just relax."

The next morning, after no great nightmares and no inspiration to change anything, I called the real estate office at the club and spoke to a Billy Richard.

"Billy, we're thinking of selling and would like to get together to talk to you."

"Today?" Billy asked.

"At your convenience," I replied.

"Then what do you say to 2:00 PM this afternoon?"

"That would work well." I hung up.

"Doris," I yelled into the bedroom where she was still getting dressed, "I've asked Billy Richard to come around at 2:00 PM this afternoon to talk about listing the house."

"I'll be there," she replied. "What about the lawyer?"

"I'll try him right away," I replied.

I picked up the phone.

"Hello?"

"Hello. May I speak to James Macready, please?"

"Speaking."

"Mr. Macready, my name is Derick Anderson, and I'm calling about some representation for a real estate transaction."

"Are you the people interested in buying the Primrose Inn? Mandy Bliss told me that you might call."

Now I knew for certain that Versailles was a small town, where everybody knew what was going on. "Yes, we are those people," I said, laughing. "Do you have time to look out for our interests if we go though with the deal?"

"Be happy to," he said. "My family is kin to folks who owned that property when it was a private home. Where do you stand at present?"

"We've got an appraisal but haven't made an offer yet. Our mortgage broker tells us that we won't have a problem getting financing."

"Okay. Can you send me a copy of the appraisal?"

"I'll try."

"And I'll look over everything before we get in touch with each. Don't sign anything until I've seen it."

"Thank you, Mr. Macready."

"Call me Jim," he said, before we hung up.

I called Henry and asked if he could send a copy of the appraisal to me and to James Macready.

"No problem," he said. "Emails are on their way right now."

I did some Internet searches on current interest rates and came away as puzzled as I had been before I started. There seemed to be so many ways to get financing with variable this and fixed that, I just prayed that Henry had our best interests at heart when he negotiated with the bank in Lexington. I couldn't find anything better from what I understood over the Internet.

Billy Richard, the island real estate guy, showed up in his oversized, real estate agent required, imported automobile. Why do those folks feel that they have to be seen driving outrageously expensive cars? I wondered. Especially on our island. He could have gotten his job done on a bicycle. The speed limit, which is strictly enforced, is 25 miles per hour and nothing is more than 5 miles away. However, here he was with his behemoth parked in our driveway, and in he walked with sheaves of papers and a huge smile on his face.

We sat around the dining room table and Billy shared his first package with us. This was a listing of all the homes that had sold on the island over the last six months. He had highlighted houses comparable in size and age to ours.

"Your house appears to be in excellent condition," he commented, peering around. "And you have a good location."

Billy's next sheaf was listings of houses that were currently on the market. They don't allow "for sale" signs outside houses on the island, but they do get listed in the multi-listing thing, and Billy had printed out what was currently available. Again, he had highlighted anything that looked like ours.

"Not a lot of competition," he noted.

The third and last list wasn't shared with us, just held up for us so that we could note its existence.

"This is a list that we keep at the club of interested parties. By that I mean people who have visited here either on vacation or otherwise and have come into the real estate office to find out what is available for sale. If there is nothing in their range, we ask to keep their name and address so that we can contact them when homes do become available that match what they're looking for."

"I've heard about it," I told Billy. "How do we fit with what folks are looking for?"

"Surprisingly well," Billy told us. "There is a good chance that if you price the home sensibly, we can move it in a matter of days."

"What do you suggest as an asking price?" I looked at him, and without hesitation, he came up with exactly the number that I was hoping for.

"Billy, you've given us good news, and I think good advice. Will you leave us to talk about it overnight, and we'll get back with you tomorrow?"

"Sure will," Billy said, and with that he was gone.

"I should have gone into real estate," I told Doris after Billy left. "It seems pretty simple stuff to me."

"Derick, you don't know the half. Anyway, you are about to become an innkeeper, aren't you?"

"It's looking more like it. Doris, are you really sure it's what you want? I'm beginning to have wet feet."

"Derick, you're that one who keeps reminding us that we have to change our lifestyle. I'm more than up to the challenge, and I do want to live closer to the children."

"Okay, but let's wait until tomorrow before we call Billy. Don't want to look too eager—they recognize that, you know."

"I love you, Derick," Doris said, shaking her head, "but you do sometimes live in a world that is all your own. Miller time, and then let's go to the club for the last supper—or one of the last suppers at least."

The next morning, Billy actually called us quite early. He told us that he had gotten on the phone after he'd left us, and that if we listed the house at the price suggested he had a potential buyer already. The prospective buyer was not too far away, in Charlotte, and wanted a vacation place on the beach. He would drive down in the next couple of days and look the place over. Doris and I were in agreement, so I told Billy to cycle over and we were ready to sign. Billy didn't seem to understand what I meant by cycling over. The poor boy probably couldn't imagine life without his behemoth.

The papers were drawn up and signed. I told Doris that we could take a chance and make an offer on the inn before selling the house. Doris told me that a few days were not going to make any difference, and that we should wait until we had the bird in our hand. She was right, of course, so I filled my time by walking the beach and wondering at times why we were leaving paradise. When I got back home and saw yellow tape around the seventeenth green, I remembered.

The prospective buyers only took two days to drive down. Apparently, we found out later, they didn't intend to move into the house but wanted it as an investment and were going to put it on the rental program run by the club. So much for the real estate talk about a perfect weekend vacation retreat. All of these things confused me, and I had thoughts that this was all some conspiracy to get the house at a rock bottom price. Maybe I wasn't thinking clearly or making the right decisions. But when the offer came, there was enough cash there to allow us to move on and have a little to spare for anything unexpected.

"Can I call now with an offer for the inn?" I asked Doris.

"What are you going to offer?"

"What we discussed, $1,100,000."

"Are you sure that that isn't too high?"

"Dolly, I'm no expert here, but I think that it will get us the inn, and we can afford it now with the house selling at the price we wanted."

"We haven't sold this one yet."

"No, but we have an offer we'll accept."

"Go for it then."

That was it. No more discussion.

I called Miles in the early evening and told him that we were considering making an offer on the inn. I was trying to be cool and not show any emotion in my voice.

"How do I go about it?" I asked.

"Tell me your offer," he replied.

"$1,100,000 turnkey."

"Make it $1,150,000 and I'll call the Detroit connection and start their seven days."

"Is $1,150,000 close to where they stand?" I asked.

"Put it this way—it's close enough that they will have to move."

"Okay Miles," I said. "$1,150,000 turnkey; I'll get it to you in writing."

"Actually, I'll send you a contract by fax, which you can sign and fax back to me."

"Okay."

The fax arrived almost immediately, and I sent a copy to Jim Macready. Jim must not have been the busiest lawyer in Kentucky because I heard back from him almost within the hour.

"Got the appraisal yesterday and got your fax this morning. The appraisal really glows, you know. You could probably read it in a dark room without turning on the light, but if it is good for the bank, okay. Eight and a half percent is a reasonable rate for today's market. The offer is standard. If the numbers are where you want them, sign it and let the dance begin."

"What dance?"

"The one between a buyer and a seller of property. I love watching that dance. Keep me in the picture."

I looked again at the fax, signed it, and Doris did, too. I dialed the number for Historic Primrose Inn and without any more thought, offered to buy something for over one million dollars. This was a milestone in my little adventure through life.

"We're in our seven-day hiatus," I told Doris after the fax was sent. "Actually, it could be less than seven days if they decide to just give up."

It was a long seven days. The Detroit people didn't give up—and must have been desperately struggling to move their house or get a bridge loan or anything from someplace. After it was over, I felt quite sorry for them. However, during the seven-day wait, I didn't like them one little bit. I don't think that I slept more than three hours a night during that week, and in the end when we got notification from Miles that the Detroit couple had withdrawn their offer and the inn was ours, I was so sleep deprived that everything seemed anticlimactic.

I remembered an old movie about electing a new pope, and how it took days and days without a majority and no white smoke. Then in the end, when the decision had been made and everybody was happy, there was a scene where the unexpected newly elected pontiff was shown saying to himself, "What do I do now? I'm the same man today as I was yesterday." I told this to Doris, who just stared at me.

"What has buying a bed and breakfast got to do with being elected Pope?" she wanted to know.

"Well, nothing," I said. "I guess that we've just committed to all this money and, oh hell, I don't know what I mean."

"I don't want to be married to a Pope," Doris said.

"Popes don't get married," I replied.

"Then I don't want to be married to a man who wants to be a Pope. Talk about delusions of grandeur."

"I'm sorry, Dolly. Maybe all's well that ends well."

"Are you thinking about being William Shakespeare now?"

Sometimes, I thought, I should just keep my mouth shut.

Everything came together, and in two weeks time we had sold our South Carolina home and bought Historic Primrose Inn. Movers had been contacted and closing dates arranged. We would have to store our furniture for a while but were told by the moving company that they would store it in Cincinnati so an easy delivery could be made to Versailles when we were ready.

The understanding that we had with Catherine and Miles was that we would move into the inn for a week and try to rotate spending at least one night in each guest room to get the general feel for the rooms. During the day, they would show us the ropes, how they managed the inn, and how they kept the books.

Catherine and Miles had their own attorney who worked out of an office in Lexington. Apparently, he had some ties with Miles in the past, and Miles wanted him involved with this transaction. Jim Macready had been kept in the picture; he had advised on and approved of all the steps that we were taking.

All the paperwork was signed and our belongings packed to be shipped out of South Carolina. We established a bank account with Jim Macready's help in Versailles and transferred our fortune electronically in order for everything to be in place in Kentucky for the closing on the inn.

We packed the car with personal items needed for the next few days and headed north to our new life. As we pulled out, I noticed that the new greens were just beginning to color up. Apparently, they were responding well to their twice-daily bath in semi-salty water. I was thrilled for them.

After an uneventful journey, our first night was spent back in the attic room where we'd stayed before. It felt different this time. Miles actually helped me unpack our car, as he had on our last visit, and I made myself promise to take Doris's advice and be nice to him.

"Would you care to join us for a drink before dinner?" Catherine asked.

"We'd love to," answered Doris. Those two women were going to hit it off, and that was going to make the whole transition thing easier.

At 5:00 PM, we joined them in the parlor. Miles offered us wine. Apparently, he was quite a self-appointed authority on wines, but we opted for a cocktail each, not caring whether we disappointed him.

"I've typed up a schedule for the next two weeks," Miles announced, and he produced a sheet of paper for each of us to review. It was organized but didn't include everything that I wanted, so I asked if we could make some changes and additions.

"Of course, dear boy," he said, nodding. "I'm glad that you're getting into the spirit of it. What changes do you suggest?"

"One of the things is that I want to spend more time with the staff and find out what they do on a daily basis."

"Oh, the staff. Well, you haven't officially met them yet. Both say that they will stay on to help you through the transition. But after that, Grayson wants to think it over. Linda desperately needs a job, so she will no doubt want to continue. I should have put that on the list."

"It would have been high on my list, Miles," I said. "There is a lot of work they do here. I'm getting on in years; I don't want to do it but do want an understanding of what it entails."

"But they are only the staff," Miles said. "The inn will run without them."

"No, it won't," Catherine said, joining in. "Time with the staff most certainly needs to be added to the list. You need to understand that Miles has never cleaned a room, made a bed, or cut the lawn since he came here."

"Pretty good gig you've got going here, Miles. Are you sure that you want to give it up?" I soon shut up because I noticed Doris glaring at me out of the corner of my eye.

"Tomorrow for the staff then," Catherine concluded.

"There may be more requests," I added, "as the week goes along and we find out more."

"Of course." Catherine was taking control now.

Catherine went on. "If you don't mind, we tend to eat very late in the evening, and we thought that you would appreciate time by yourselves at the end of each day. So we haven't made any dinner plans until after the closing when we want to treat you to the best meal in the area."

"That is just perfect, Catherine, thank you," I said. "Miles, is everything on track to close on time?"

"It is, dear boy. Well, maybe a hitch here and a hitch there—our attorney doesn't understand that he has to do as I say, not doing what he says. But we'll survive."

Oh no, I thought, *that sounds like a delay to me*.

We went back to Mandy's for dinner. She had a prime rib special, which was fabulous. The restaurant was very busy, probably because of the special, so we didn't see Mandy. Her mother wasn't there either.

Back to the inn, back to the attic, we set the alarm for 6:30 AM and climbed into bed for a good night's rest.

The next morning, we were up, showered, and dressed for the day and reported to the kitchen at 7:15 AM—fifteen minutes earlier than the start time on Miles's list.

Catherine was preparing eggs for scrambling and Miles was filling his little bottles of juice.

"Morning," we said. "Any coffee on the go?"

"Always coffee," Miles mumbled, still obviously disappointed that we didn't prefer morning tea.

I watched him dilute the frozen orange concentrate and thought he must have been mixed up when he diluted it four to one instead of the usual three to one. But this was just the first of many little things that I observed about the various way Miles had adopted to keep his bottom line healthy. I was going to get an education after all.

It was time to chop the fruit. With great flourish, Miles chopped grapes in half, quartered strawberries, pealed and cut up oranges—all were mixed in a bowl and left while he got on with other things.

Catherine, still busy with her eggs, had also prepared a French toast concoction in heart-shaped ramekins. Miles carried in an enormous packet of bacon from one of the refrigerators. The bacon was packed in layers of nine pieces to a sheet, and he proceeded to place one layer onto a paper lined cookie sheet ready for the oven. Miles was going to bake the bacon.

"It doesn't shrink quite so much when baked," Miles explained.

The first guests showed up at 8:30 AM, and Miles hopped off into the dining room to seat them and generally fuss around. In truth, it was a relief to have him leave the kitchen where he had been acting like the master chef, but a master chef with no real authority. It was going to be a long week.

Miles hopped back into the kitchen, then hopped through the kitchen to a closet where the stereo was located. He had an iPod, which he plugged into it, and soon there were sounds of classical music floating throughout the house. I liked that.

Catherine was in charge of the plating, and Doris helped her. Breakfast looked good. A heart-shaped piece of French toast, scrambled eggs, and bacon. Miles had to approve each plate before it left the kitchen, but it was only a gesture. One got the feeling that if he offered any criticism, Catherine would have put him into his place.

I wandered into the dining room to observe and must say people did look at Miles as if he were off the wall and some sort of loose cannon that might go off without warning. However breakfast went well—two sittings, one at 8:30 AM and the other at 9:00 AM. The inn was not full and could easily have sat everybody at either time, but I was impressed that they allowed some flexibility in the time for the meal.

After the meal, most guests returned to their rooms to pack if they were leaving or to otherwise get ready for their day. Miles and I cleared the tables, rinsed off the dirty dishes, and placed them in the sink for soaking ready for the dishwasher. There were two dishwashers and one had a pool of standing water near its drain.

"What's the matter with this?" I asked Miles.

"Nothing's the matter," he replied. "There has to be water there to keep the seals moist."

I'd never heard if that.

Bookkeeping was not on our schedule for that day, and even though I wanted to move along with this whole training process, I didn't want to rock the boat, and I especially didn't want to get Doris upset. We helped where we could in the kitchen and then made our way to the parlor to say goodbye to those guests who were leaving.

As the guests headed out, the staff headed in. First was Grayson George. Grayson drove a sensible car—something Japanese; I've never been good at telling them apart. This morning he wore a wooly hat that said "Niagara Falls" on the front. He opened the trunk of his car in the parking lot and pulled out an oversized jump suit, which he proceeded to climb into. I just couldn't figure him out and worried that I might never figure him out—and I was about to employ him.

He walked around to the back and entered the house through the kitchen door.

"Morning," he almost shouted.

"Good morning, Grayson," Catherine answered. "How are you? You remember the Andersons, don't you?"

He hardly looked at us, just nodded and helped himself to a cup of coffee.

We all stood mute, and something was needed to break the ice. So right on cue and as if by magic, we heard it—bang hiss cough, cough rumble, rumble, rumble—and the derelict old car that we had seen on our previous visit was pulling itself into a parking space next to where Grayson had parked. It stopped and then went through the same shuddering routine as previously.

"That's Linda's ride," Catherine told us, and we waited to see who was going to emerge from the *la machina*. Nothing happened.

"Is she all right?" I asked.

"Oh yes," Catherine responded. "She likes to smoke a cigarette before she gets out of the car. Must be like some sort of hell in there," she added.

In time, surrounded by a great creaking noise as she opened the door, out stepped Linda. Dear lord what a sight. Slightly overweight, maybe, but difficult to tell for sure because she was wrapped up in several layers of clothing. A wooly hat like Grayson's but without a logo on it, and oversized boots looking way too big for her feet.

More creaking and squeaking as she slammed the door closed and like Grayson, she headed for the back door. Once inside, off came the hat and her hair was all over the place. She smiled at us and displayed a remarkable lack of teeth. Her skin was darkish but not black.

"Good morning, Linda," Catherine said.

Linda had a little nervous laugh that we later learned precedes most things that she says. "Ha, ha, ha, good morning."

She went to the refrigerator and looked at an attached whiteboard of a list of tasks that needed to be done that day. Apparently, Catherine had prepared the list earlier.

"Linda, these are the Andersons," Catherine said. "You remember we talked about them? They are going to want to talk to you to see if you want to go on working here after they buy the inn."

"Ha, ha..." Again the nervous laugh.

I joined in the conversation. "We also want to find out what you do," I added.

Linda didn't even look at me. She went on studying her list, poured a cup of coffee, then wandered outside to join Grayson—and smoke another cigarette.

She's very shy when meeting new people," Catherine explained.

Doris and I just looked at each other, not knowing what to think.

"We have to talk to them at some time," Doris suggested.

"Let's not rush it," I replied. "Maybe they need to get used to us before they open up. We do represent a major change in their lives."

The week progressed at what seemed like a snail's pace. Because we thought we wanted to experience what each room was like, Doris and I moved to a different room each night. This was a mistake because we had to drag our things with us each time we moved. Most likely, we didn't actually need to *sleep* in the room to get a feel for it.

From time to time, we talked with Grayson, and more and more with Linda. Catherine told us that she thought that Linda was an almost full-blooded Cherokee, and that in the summer she would sometimes wear her hair in plaits that made her look very much like an Indian maid.

I couldn't figure out what Grayson did each day. He certainly looked the part with a different outfit for each task. He had a good supply of orange cones, and they would be placed around, moved, then placed in different places as he worked his way around outside the house. His rubber hammer was usually at hand.

We *could* figure out what Linda did, and she actually worked hard. Every time a guest left a room, Linda stripped the bed, washed the sheets, and made the bed back up. She also vacuumed and dusted each room and the common rooms as directed. There were frequent cigarette breaks, and she consumed an enormous amount of coffee. Our main problem with her was that she was very hard to understand. I tried joking about my not speaking "Kentucky," but she was probably having just as much trouble understanding me.

Doris spent time with Catherine learning how she prepared menus and made out foolproof shopping lists for Miles.

I was figuring Miles out, too, and concluded that he was all bustle without a lot of substance. Catherine was the driving force behind just about everything in the inn. She planned the menus and did most of the cooking. She did all of the bookkeeping and saw to it that money was collected and bills paid. She did allow Miles to do the heavy shopping, but on each occasion before leaving the house, he was reminded to stay to the list and add "nothing creative."

We didn't go back to Mandy's again during that week, figuring that we needed to become familiar with the other restaurants in the area. But we missed Mandy's, and it certainly stood out in our minds as a place to send guests who were looking for casual good food.

I was learning the books, learning how to make reservations, and learning how to process credit cards. Some things that I thought would be easy turned out to be much more complicated than anticipated, but I did become convinced that whatever Catherine and Miles were doing didn't have to be so cluttered. The computer system, like the house, had so many attachments and back ups it made one's head hurt just to think about them. As the week went on, I determined that as soon as we took over, I would hire a bookkeeper and keep the books off site, upgrade the reservation system so that reservations could flow in automatically, and get an answering service with real people instead of the machines that were used at the inn presently.

Day five, and disaster struck. Something had happened between Miles and his attorney and the closing would need to be postponed. Catherine was apologetic, but whatever had happened was out of her control.

"I'm so sorry," she said. "Maybe I should have warned you that things sometimes go a little astray when Miles gets involved. It won't be anything big, just enough to worry him and make him act foolishly. We maybe need a couple of extra days to sort it out."

"Catherine," I replied, "sort it out with him, please. Don't let me get involved. I might not be responsible for anything I say or do. Doris and I will go and spend some time with either Lower C or Middle C and wait until you're ready. Just don't drag it out too long."

"No more than a few days, I promise," she said.

"I know," I answered.

I called Jim Macready to let him know of the delay, but he was ahead of me. "There's an outside chance that Miles and his attorney might actually duke it out before this is over," he told us. "Perhaps we can sell tickets. I know what the problem is; it's absolutely a non-issue and will be put right in no time."

"Well, we're going away for a day or two," I said to Jim.

"Stay in touch, and use me as the trigger to come back," he said. "I'll keep them on track."

I was beginning to like Jim Macready a lot, and I was grateful to Mandy for recommending him.

I called Alec. "Can we come and crash for a couple of days?" I asked. "It might just save your father from a prison sentence for murder. I don't think that I could get away with a plea of justifiable homicide, so I need not to be here."

"Sure Pop. I'm not sure what that is all about, but come on by anytime."

Off we went to Ohio. We called both other boys to let them know what was going on, but we didn't want to bother them, as we were going to need their help when we eventually moved into the inn.

Alec and Mary were just the same—one bouncing off the wall and the other sitting quietly through it trying to behave as if all was peaceful and calm.

"They're not going to make it; you do know this, don't you?" Doris said to me. "We should be happy that there are no children involved."

"You say that every time," I answered. "Alec *is* the child."

"True," Doris said. "You know, he might always be a child."

"I love him to death, and I love Mary, too."

"Well, Alec thinks the world of you. Mary, on the other hand, has a great respect but, I believe, is starting to blame us for Alec's immaturity."

"If it goes bust, we'll have a place for him at the inn."

"No we won't—other than one day, maybe two once in a while. If he keeps running back to us, he'll never grow up and accept responsibility."

"But I love him."

"It's got to be tough love from now on."

We visited our old haunts in and around Columbus and spent some time with friends. However, in spite of having a good time, we were getting antsy about not hearing from somebody in Kentucky regarding what was going on.

I was all for driving back there and having it out with Miles. I'm not a physically big person, but I could certainly get a few whacks in on that little squirt. Doris preached the waiting game, at least for few days, and as usual, she was right.

First on the phone was Jim Macready. "We're all set up for closing the day after tomorrow. Can you guys make it back here for that?"

"Sure can, Jim," I answered. "Nothing has changed, has it?"

"Not from our perspective," he said. "The other party has made some changes to their arrangements, but we remain the same. Same money, same everything."

"Jim, I'm right in thinking that once we sign, we're the ones making decisions and setting rules and regulations."

"Yes, you're right."

"Can the closing be later in the day?"

"We can make it at 3:00 PM if you wish."

"Good. Doris and I will drive down from Ohio that morning."

"See you then. Call if you have questions."

The next call was from Miles.

"I've sorted those rascals out and got this business squared away," Miles announced in his increasingly annoying pompous way. "We can now proceed to closing."

"Miles, I understand that we are on for 3:00 PM the day after tomorrow in Jim Macready's office, is that right?"

"No, I haven't determined that yet."

"Miles, is Catherine there?"

"Yes she is. Do you want a word?"

"Please."

A moment later, Catherine picked up. "Hello, Derick."

"Hello to you, love," I said. "Look, don't take this the wrong way, but something is very wrong and needs to be put out of its misery."

"How can I help?"

She was so nice, but surely she already knew exactly what the problem was.

"The closing is set up for 3:00 PM the day after tomorrow. We plan on staying in Ohio until then, so we'll meet you in Jim Macready's office at that time. After the closing, and after you have signed everything over to us, I want nothing more to do with Miles. I would prefer that he be out of the inn and out of my life. He is an incredible disruption."

"You want us to move out that day, Derick?" Catherine was hurt.

"Not you, Catherine—just Mr. High and Mighty. Although I do understand that you come as a package. Would you block off one of the rooms for Doris and me, and can you try to have your personal possessions out of the inn before we come back after the closing?"

"Derick, in truth, Miles doesn't even need to be at the closing. The inn belongs to me and to me alone. He just feels this need to protect me. That is why he is so disruptive."

"Catherine, again, you are magnificent. I've already learned a lot from you and delight in your company, but Miles has buggered up things one time too many, if you'll excuse me. No more Miles. Maybe he can orchestrate your move out while the rest of us are signing papers?"

"I'm sorry, Derick," Catherine said, sighing.

"I'm sorry, too, but if we don't close at 3:00 PM the day after tomorrow, we don't close. I honestly think we've bent as much as we can."

"You have, Derick. I'll do what I can do."

"Let us know."

"I will, but I'm guessing that everything will proceed as planned for 3:00 PM the day after tomorrow."

When I got off the phone, Doris wanted to know what was going on.

"Well, we close on the inn at 3:00 PM the day after tomorrow, and I've just peed a little higher up the wall," I said.

"What?"

"It's a guy thing. I've put a crimp into the style of the little pip squeak, that's all."

"Is there going to be trouble?"

"Who knows."

SEMI-RETIREMENT

* * *

The next day, Catherine called to let me know that Miles would not be at the closing at all and that they had made arrangements for them to move in with one of her children, who was local to the area. She was sorry that she wouldn't be able to get their furniture and personal belongings out of the inn until after the closing, but they themselves would be gone.

"I really appreciate that, Catherine," I told her. "And we will see you tomorrow at 3:00 PM. By the way, is there a weekend coming up soon when the inn won't be busy?"

"Oh yes, at this time of year, traffic is slow."

"How about the weekend after next?"

"Let me see, yes, that looks pretty clear."

"Would you block it off for me, please? It might be a good time for us to get our furniture moved in."

I heard some clicks. "It's done," Catherine said. "See you tomorrow."

"It's all coming together at last," I told Doris, when I got off the phone. "We're on for the closing tomorrow, and I've asked Catherine to block off the weekend after next so that we can get moved in. I'll call High C and Lower C tonight to see if they can come down to help. I'm sure that Alec will be there. He's itching to see the place—thinks he'll make a good innkeeper!"

After I'd called both other boys and their families everyone indicated that they were more than happy to come down to Kentucky and help us move in. The moving truck would arrive the Friday ahead of the weekend that we wanted. The truck would then be left to be picked up empty Monday morning.

"We're cooking with gas," I told Doris.

"Sometimes, you are as immature as your middle son," she replied.

***

It was a pleasant, non-hurried drive down the next day. I had put on a tie in recognition of the fact that I would soon be signing checks for more than one million dollars.

"Now Derick, you are okay with not doing one final look-through on the house before we sign?" Jim Macready asked, as we all assembled in Jim Macready's office.

"Is everything okay?" I asked Catherine.

"It is," she replied.

"Then her word is good enough for us, isn't it, Doris?"

"Of course," Doris said, with a nice smile in Catherine's direction.

From there, it couldn't have gone any smoother or easier. We simply signed and signed form after form and finally, we were handed the keys.

Outside Jim's office, Catherine said, "You have two couples who checked in yesterday and will be leaving in the morning, and then two more checking in tomorrow. You should find plenty of everything in the 'fridge and pantry. Grayson and Linda have both been to work today; they will have left by now, but both are coming tomorrow. Miles and I are spending tonight and the rest of our time in Kentucky at my son's. We leave for Florida in about a week."

"Thank you for everything, Catherine," I said. I was a little worried in that she was starting to look sad.

"Are you okay?" I asked Catherine.

'It's a big move for me, too, Derick," she replied, "but I'll be all right."

CHAPTER 7

Moving In

The inn was quiet. There was nobody there; we couldn't believe it.

"Would you like a glass of wine?" I asked Doris.

"Oh, no thanks. Why don't we just walk around and share thoughts on what changes we want to make."

"That works for me. I've got a hundred ideas."

Mostly what we wanted to do was get rid of clutter. The inn was overfull with "stuff" and whereas that might be one way of interpreting how the Victorians decorated, it just wasn't us. We preferred cleaner lines and more space.

I also wanted an end to the various money saving tricks, such as over-diluting the orange juice. Doris agreed. In fact, Doris suggested that we rethink the whole way that we present breakfast.

"Back in the day," Doris explained, "in those grand old houses in England when they had their weekend get-togethers, breakfast was usually served buffet style. A true English gentleman is not served at breakfast," Doris reminded me. "The usual set up is for dishes on a sideboard, and host and guests alike serve themselves to whatever they want."

"Do you think that would work for us here?"

"Maybe, but probably not. We could adopt some of those ideas—especially for the juices and maybe some breakfast breads. Coffee, too. That would save us from having to run around making sure that everybody gets what they want. If we can't get to them, they can help themselves."

"I'm not sure that I understand."

"Well, Mr. New Innkeeper, we would put one of the coffee burners in the dining room, and if we haven't had the chance to go around and offer topping up, the guests could simple help themselves. Plus, we set out decanters of orange juice and cranberry juice so that guests can serve themselves just what they want, and that way we wouldn't get so many half-finished glasses returned."

"Good thinking, Doris. You know, we might just have an affinity for this business."

"It's early days, and let's not run before we can walk." She shook her head. "You are acting like Alec. What is it Mary says? 'It's quiet time; time to think the thing through.'"

"We have our first breakfast alone tomorrow," I reminded Doris. "Are you looking forward to it?"

"You know, I am. Only four people, right?"

"Right."

Everything went fine the next morning. We just continued in the way that Miles and Catherine had shown us and didn't put any of our new changes into effect. The guests seemed happy, and all the food got eaten.

After we cleared up, Doris sat down armed with new recipe books to go over her menus while I went to the computer for my first solo flight with the reservation software. It was difficult piloting my way through the different aspects of the system without the comforting voice of Catherine behind me saying, "Are you sure that you want to do that?" But I was determined not to be intimidated by the wretched machine and was quite lost to the world, staring at the screen and testing various commands, when a voice coming from just behind my shoulder made me jump out of my skin.

"How much money did you make from the gift shop when the guests checked out this morning?"

I twisted around in my seat. It was Miles.

"God, Miles, you scared the hell out of me. Can't you knock or something, instead of creeping up on people?"

"Better get used to it," he said. "The public think that they own this public house and can walk around where and whenever they like."

"They can, Miles. You can't!"

"I heard that the closing went well. I was just too busy to be there. As I told Catherine just yesterday morning, 'I think that we have gone as far as we can with the Andersons and it's time to cut them loose and let them get on with it.'"

Did he really believe that? Who was to know? I didn't believe him for a moment, but somehow, it now seemed to me that when Catherine had put it to him that he was a persona non grata at the closing, he had somehow converted that as it being all his idea. The man was certifiably crazy, and I was feeling more and more sorry for Catherine.

"What is that you want, Miles?" I asked.

"Dear boy, this afternoon I have a team of Mexicans coming here to move our furniture and the other personal items that we've discussed out of the house. We might not have room for everything, and I'm prepared to make you a good price on anything that we leave behind."

"Miles, there is already too much stuff in the inn. If you haven't organized a big enough truck, maybe you can get your Mexicans to stack the overage in the barn or at the end of the drive. I'm not giving you any more money than I already have, and if we do store it for you, I'm charging a fee."

"Nothing that you want?" he asked.

"Not a single thing."

Doris showed up at the library office door, and she, too, was a little taken aback to see Miles.

"Is there something wrong?" she asked.

"No, dear woman," he said, straightening up to his full height. "I'm merely here to organize an orderly collection of our personal effects."

"He means that he has a group of non-English-speaking Mexicans coming around this afternoon to cart away his crap," I said. "What time will they be here, Miles?"

"Two thirty."

"Good, then we'll see you then." I put an end to the conversation.

It was his turn now to be a little taken aback, but give credit where credit is due, he nodded, looked around the room at nothing in particular, took a deep breath, and left.

When he was gone, I looked at Doris and said, "He just walked in, stood looking over my shoulder, and started to talk to me. He said that it was all his idea about not showing up at the closing and putting an end to our orientation. I can't stand the little pip squeak."

"Derick, please promise that you will do nothing that you will regret for the next week or so until they have left for Florida."

"I promise, no homicide," I said, holding up my hands. "Although I was wrong in what I said to Alec. Any reasonable jury knowing the facts would call it justifiable homicide. I'm sorry, Doris. I'll be good."

A U-Haul truck showed up in the driveway just after 2:30 PM. I was surprised to find out that I had been correct about the Mexicans not speaking very much English. The leader of the group, who went by the name of Arturo, did speak my native tongue but with a wickedly thick accent. He was such an upbeat and happy guy that it didn't seem to matter that one could only understand every other word he said, and it certainly didn't bother him. He rattled on like a steam engine.

It turns out that Arturo, who works at one of the horse farms and is in the country quite legally, also organizes casual labor for his "friends" and neighbors—laborers who maybe are not here quite so legally.

There is a large Mexican population in Versailles because of the horse industry. There seems to be the perception that Mexicans have a natural affinity to working with horses. Later, I would come to suspect that it probably also had something to do with them working for next to nothing. Miles had used Arturo's connections in the past and without doubt got them on the cheap. I would later take advantage of this connection, too, and I got to love their restaurants, where no English is spoken.

In no time the truck was loaded, even though Miles was up to his usual antics of telling the workers where everything had to be placed. But as he was probably paying the group by the hour, he may not have wanted unnecessary delays.

As they were leaving, I asked Arturo to drop around the inn at his convenience, that I might have some business for him.

"You are a lucky man to have me to share all these little tips and money saving ideas with you, aren't you?" Miles said to me.

"Miles, I'm so lucky, I could just shit." Oh, how this man got on my nerves, and he brought out the very worst in me.

Doris and I spent most of our waking moments over the next few days discussing and planning the changes that we had in mind for the inn. First, there was the furniture—how were we going to move it around so that the worst of the junk that we had inherited got thrown out and the rest was used to maximum advantage? How were we going to change the menus? What to do about the gift shop? What to do with the reservation software and how to keep the books?

We were fortunately quiet with regard to guests during this period. Grayson and Linda came every day and somehow managed to find things to do. We had only the briefest of conversations with them, which might have been because we didn't want to get too involved until Doris and I had a clear idea of our direction—also, until we knew that Miles and Catherine had finally left town. I suspected that Grayson was seeing Miles and Catherine either on his way to work or on his way home. I didn't want him passing on anything to them, so I chose not to share our thoughts.

I asked Linda about her car.

She started with her typical nervous laugh.

"My honey got me this car; it's a real doosy, ain't it?"

"It's a doosy all right. How does it run for you? Is it reliable?"

She shook her head. "Ha ha ha . . . No, it ain't."

One only had short conversations with Linda—more a series of statements than conversations.

Alec telephoned and said that he was coming a few days early, but Mary couldn't come early so she wasn't coming at all.

"It's the beginning of the end for those two," observed Doris. "I'm telling you."

There was one little hiccup during the week of waiting for the furniture. We had a guest booked in for a couple of nights who managed to get lost trying to find us. She telephoned and asked for directions, and I helped as well as I could but still didn't know my own way around very well. When she eventfully showed up, Doris tried to be especially nice to make up for our newness and inability to help her find her way.

Doris decided that an offer of wine might help the situation and asked the guest if she would like a glass.

"That would be nice. Do you have a cold Sauvignon Blanc?"

"I'm sure that we do," Doris said. "Derick, will you open a bottle of Sauvignon Blanc, please?"

I was totally caught off guard. My eyes opened really wide and my eyebrows arched well into my forehead. I indicated with a nod and flash of eyes for Doris to join me in the kitchen.

"What bottle of Sauvignon Blanc are you talking about?" I asked.

"All that wine in the basement," Doris said. "There must be a bottle of Sauvignon Blanc in with all of that."

"That was Miles's wine, and he has taken it away with him."

"How was I to know that? You'd better go and buy one."

"Where?"

"There's that liquor store just down the hill. You could walk there."

"It's a drive-thru, Doris. They sell beer and cigarettes."

"Oh, but the sign in their window says wine." Doris was being very persistent.

I knew that I had to go, but I decided not to walk. I ran for the car and drove down Rose Hill Avenue.

I pulled into the passageway beside the store and up to the drive-thru window. It was very murky in there, and I could smell cigarette smoke through the open window. A man's face was staring at me.

"Do you have a cold Sauvignon Blanc?" I asked.

"Eh?" he said.

"A cold bottle of Sauvignon Blanc," I asked again.

Another "Eh." Perhaps my accent was confusing him.

"Cold white wine," I said, trying a different approach.

"Eh."

"Can I come in and look?" I asked, and he nodded.

I parked behind the shop and ran the wrong way back down their driveway, passing the window and confusing the customer who had pulled in behind me. I pushed at their door, which had an "Open" sign displayed, but it wouldn't move. I knocked, and in a while, the gentleman who I had been talking to through the window came forward with a bottle of wine in one hand and keys in the other.

"We've got this," he said, and handed me a bottle of Merlot that was frozen cold. "Is this what you're looking for?"

"Not exactly," I replied. "Can I come in and look around?"

"Eh, oh yes."

The place was quite a, what we describe in England as a tip—beer cases somewhat haphazardly lying around and cartons of cigarettes with a few boxes of cigars.

"Where would I find the wine?"

I was directed to a dirty cooler that had a few more bottles of Merlot and some shelves with an assortment of other bottles of all sorts. On top of the cooler at room temperature I found a bottle of Chablis covered in a sticky dust that one gets from cigarette smoke—the only white wine that I could see in the shop.

"I'll take this please," I said to the man. He nodded and asked for $7.50.

With that, I rushed back to my car and rushed back up the hill.

Doris was engaged in conversation with our new guest and gave me a look that meant, "Help me! Where have you been!" when I got back into the room.

"The Sauvignon Blanc must have been taken as hostage by somebody," I said. "How about something retro? I haven't had Chablis for years." I was trying to keep everything light.

Our guest nodded in agreement. "That sounds fine."

"Then let's really go back to the good old days and drink it over ice."

I didn't wait for an answer. I jumped back into the kitchen and attacked the bottle. I did catch a break in that there was a screw off top to the bottle. I'm sure as old as this was, and that as it had been standing upright on that shelf for years, that the cork would have broken when I tried to open it. I screwed off the top and thought that I noticed a little fizz, but I ignored it. I quickly found three wine glasses, filled them with ice—too much, but what the hell at this stage. I poured some wine over the ice and now was positive that there was a fizz thing going on. I put the glasses on a tray and took them to the parlor.

Doris and the guest both took a glass, and the telephone rang just as I was about to take mine.

"I'll get it," I said. There were more bad looks directly at me from Doris. The phone call was somebody making a reservation, and it took some time to get all the details down.

When I returned to the parlor, both the guest and Doris had departed. There were three almost full glasses of wine on the coffee table, and I do believe that they were still fizzing.

"Doris," I called out.

"In the kitchen," she replied. I went to join her.

"What's the story?" I asked.

"We think that your wine might have corked. Apparently, our guest is quite the authority, and she is certain that something must have happened to the cork and the wine has gone off."

"Eh," I said to Doris.

"What does that mean?" she asked.

"Well, you had to be there," I said, "but please don't offer more wine to anybody until we're set up to do it. Oh, and be sure to congratulate our guest, the great sommelier, on her diagnosis. Corked indeed! But then I guess that she hasn't ever tasted a $7.50 twist-off bottle of Chablis."

Arturo called around the next day, and we really bonded. He accepted a beer and told us about all the work that he had helped with around the inn. I still found him very difficult to understand, but I loved the twinkle in his eye whenever he told us one of his stories. He started to call Doris "Miss Doris," which we took as a sign of acceptance. We were comparing notes about our backgrounds and the fact that neither of us had been born in the United States. We were talking about food, and I thought that he was getting ready to tell me a story and was perhaps testing the water about how far he could go with using bad language.

"Do you say God and Shit?" he asked, in his thickest of thick accent. It sounded like *Gourd* and *Sheet.*

I was confused but told him, "Yes."

"So do I," he replied, "but not so much here."

What on earth was he trying to tell me? Was it that we were now living in the Bible belt, and I had to be careful about saying "God" and "Shit" in the same sentence? What did any of that have to do with our original conversation about food?

It took some time for us to figure it out, but he was not asking if I said *Gourd* and *Sheet*; he was actually asking if I *ate goat and sheep.* We laughed a lot after that, and have laughed a lot about it since.

Arturo indicated that he knew a few young men who could help us move furniture around when the van showed up next weekend. With them and the family, I thought that we were in good shape to get the inn put the way we wanted.

I also hired a fast-talking, smiley, red-headed young kid to clean the windows, inside and out. He said that he was just starting out in his new business and would make us a good price as long as we were happy with his work and would recommended him. I agreed, but only if his work warranted it. Linda told us that in the three years that she had worked at the inn, the windows had never been cleaned professionally.

Two hurdles crossed—muscle for moving furniture and a window cleaner.

Alec showed up full of enthusiasm for our new way of life and full of all the help that he was going to be. He was going to turn this inn into the premier destination in all of Kentucky—perhaps even the United States.

"How's your job going?" I asked.

"It's going," he replied, but he didn't expand further. It's not that he isn't bright—maybe he's *too* bright—it's just that he seems to always need something to be excited about, and then he throws himself into it almost to the exclusion of everything else. The latest obsession was Historic Primrose Inn, and I hoped that this old building was strong enough to stand up to everything that he had in mind to "improve" upon. I knew that Doris and I would not easily stand up to it.

"Please God that the others will dilute his enthusiasm when they get here." Doris was airing her thoughts out loud.

Move-in day minus one came around, and everything was in place. The inn had been closed off; there were no guests.

The window cleaner showed up, and I told him to go ahead and get done all that he could while there were only a few people around. I should have mentioned to Doris that the window cleaner had arrived, and I have lived to regret the omission ever since. He went about his work with great gusto—up and down his ladder and really doing an excellent job first cleaning and then shining up the old glass. I watched for a while and became convinced that I wasn't needed, so I went to find Alec and the two of us set about fixing up some games for the children to play while the adults were all busy moving furniture. I didn't see the window cleaner for a while until I almost bumped into him by accident. The young man was sitting on the back patio with a dazed look and appearing very pale.

"Are you okay?" I enquired.

"I think that I've just done a terrible thing," he replied.

"What?" I asked, but he wouldn't say anything else, he just folded back into himself and the gaunt look returned to his face.

I was confused and then heard Alec shouting for me. "You need to go find out what's wrong with Mom," he said.

I found Doris in the bedroom. She was dressed in a bathrobe and sitting in one of the side chairs. I could tell she had been crying.

"Doris," I enquired. "What is the matter?"

She stared at me, then said, "Why don't you tell people when there are strangers in the house?"

"What kind of strangers?"

"In this case, it's a red-headed young man with a bucket."

"Oh, the window cleaner," I said. "He's doing a good job, don't you think?"

"He has to leave."

"Why?"

"I just don't want to see him or to have him see me ever again."

I didn't understand. Here was Doris, distraught and looking gaunt sitting in the bedroom, and there was the window cleaner, distraught and looking gaunt sitting on the patio.

It turned out that Doris had taken the opportunity, before crowds of people showed up, to take a shower. I hadn't told anybody that window cleaning was underway, and I told the window cleaner that he could go anywhere he wanted. Of course the inevitable happened, and just when Doris was stepping out of shower, the window cleaner walked into the bathroom intent on cleaning windows there. They were both mortified, and I was in big trouble.

It was actually Alec who came to the rescue and calmed everybody down.

"Mom, it was an accident. The young guy didn't think that you were flashing him; he is just as upset as you."

"I want him to leave. I can't look him in the face ever again."

"Oh, let him finish his job. Don't they make jokes about this sort of thing happening with window cleaners all the time?"

"In your world, Alec, maybe they do, but not in mine."

"In my world, Mom, people walk around naked all the time. In fact, it is more normal to see folks' bare ass then it is to see them dressed. I've got friends whom I've never seen with clothes. I probably wouldn't recognize them if I did. Tell you what, I'll move him along and get him to come back on a day when you're not here."

"I'm not too happy with your father either."

"Nobody is happy with Pop, Mom, but we need to keep him around. We'll just throw him a bone every now and then and tell him he's a good boy."

"Alec, that is not what I mean at all."

"I know, but this is water under the bridge now and time to move on." By letting Doris vent, Alec saved the day. The young window cleaner was paid for what he had done up to that time, and arrangements were made to contact him when he could come back and finish off. I was in the dog house for an hour or so, but as so much was about to happen and as all the family were due at the inn, Doris soon calmed down and I was gently let off the hook.

High C and Lower C, along with their families, showed up on time. Games were set up to keep the children amused and the "men" sat around while I instructed them on what we wanted moved or changed or thrown away. Doris prepared a wonderful home cooked meal, we broke into our stash of beer and wine, and then replete with full tummies went to bed. It was wonderful to have this fine old house filled with our family and to hear everybody optimistic about our new venture.

The Mexicans arrived early the next morning, and although I was pleased to see them, I was a little upset that virtually no English was spoken. Arturo said not to worry, that he would take responsibility for their direction. All that we had to do was tell him what we wanted. Right on time, the moving truck arrived, and our first problem of the day arrived with it. The truck was too big to get down our driveway.

"You can order a smaller truck if you wish," the driver told us, "but it will take at least a week to take this one back and load everything off this and onto one or maybe two sixteen footers. Or, the alternative is if the neighbors don't mind, we can park out here on the street and ferry everything by hand down the driveway into the house."

"I'll check with the neighbors," Alec volunteered, and before we had the chance to discuss the pros and cons, he took off to bang on doors and rattle windows. Just the sort of thing he loves.

He was right of course; time was of the essence. We had to get unloaded that day. All was in place, and the weather was good. *Thank goodness for the Mexicans,* I thought to myself, but I knew that it was going to cost a little more than originally planned.

Linda showed up, which I thought strange since she usually didn't arrive until late morning and here she was driving the doosy up the street looking for a place to park well before 10:00 AM.

"Just want to be of help to you," she said.

"Okay," I responded, but I didn't know what she thought she could do that wasn't already covered.

Alec came back with the news that nobody had any problems with the truck being parked on the street during the day. My guess is that he really didn't give them much of a chance to say no.

"You have unusual neighbors," he told us.

How would he know?

"The funeral guy next door says that he keeps the police department informed when he has a big funeral, and it might be diplomatic for us to tell the police about the truck rather than have them find out about it from somebody else."

"Good idea," I said. "I'll call them. I need to introduce myself anyway."

"Thank you for telling us," the police officer said over the phone. "I'll make a note that you telephoned."

Everybody was gathered outside on the front lawn as I came back and announced that everything was a go. "Ask if you have questions, but let's make a start."

It was a long and tiring day. Beds were moved around from bedroom to bedroom in order to get the configurations according to the way that Doris and I had worked it out. The kitchen was rearranged and refrigerators, even one of the dishwashers, were moved to a different place based on what we thought would work best for us. Chairs and tables were brought in or taken out and placed where we wanted them. Paintings were moved and sometimes moved again. Alec in particular was deeply involved with this part of the endeavor. Some of the rugs and carpets were changed around. Everybody worked hard, sandwiches and soft drinks were made available, and there was Linda observing it all. *What is she up to*? I thought.

Finally, we were done. Arturo and his band of amigos were paid off; we tipped the truck driver and his helper, and they were gone; as for the rest of us, we were exhausted. Doris and our two daughters-in-law had taken the opportunity of being in a large, almost commercial kitchen to prepare a favorite meal from our past. It's called "Continental Meat Pie," a combination of Italian sausage, ham and salami, fresh vegetables, and lots of cheese all baked in a pastry shell. It looked good and tasted even better piping hot from the oven.

Lower C and High C were leaving first thing in the morning. They had jobs to get back to. Middle C, Alec, said he would stay on for an extra day or two just to help out.

"Don't you have to get back to work?" I asked him.

"Eventually," he replied.

CHAPTER 8

Early Days

The next day, after all the goodbyes, Doris and I settled into our new lives as innkeepers. There was still some reorganizing to be done, and maybe it was a good thing that Alec had stayed to help us. Doris worked on her menus; we had guests due to check in later in the day.

One change we had decided upon was to set up juices, yoghurt, cereal, and baked goods on the sideboard in the dining room where guests could serve themselves. We thought about putting a bowl of fruit on the sideboard as well but decided to keep serving that individually in the crystal glasses that we had inherited when we bought the inn. We thought that by doing this, it gave us a chance to interact with the guests and let them know our system of doing things. One of the coffee burners was set up on a small table in the dining room, and we placed extra coffee cups, cream, and sugar there so folks could help themselves. We also thought that we would offer choices at breakfast. They could pick bacon, sausage, or ham; scrambled or fried eggs; and these would be served with what would be a single entrée for the day, some kind of French toast or breakfast casserole. I would make up some little menus.

The computer system in place was in as much of a clutter as the rest of the house. Obviously, Catherine and Miles needed to have a back-up system for their reservation software, but as they never deleted anything, they must have been constantly running out of space. They patched that problem by buying new computers and hooking everything up together. I had learned that the company who supplied our reservation software had upgraded many things over the years and now had a service where one could keep all the reservations backed up on their computers in Texas. They called it replicating. As I am nowhere near to being proficient with computer software, and as they offered a service contract if I switched over to them, I made the switch. It was painless, and I felt a lot better knowing that I had all of that support behind me should anything go wrong.

I also contacted an old friend in Ohio for bookkeeping advice. Barbara had her own bookkeeping company, and my initial inquiry was for advice on what to do. She suggested that she look after our books for us. All that we needed to do was to mail her our receipts every week, and she would keep our books in her system so no need to worry about crashes of the computer in that area, too. We trusted Barbara and took her up on her suggestion.

Now that everything important to maintaining accurate records for the business was taken care of, I cleaned up the computers. I was proud that in no time we had everything working like clockwork, and at what now seemed like breakneck speed compared to the system that we'd inherited.

As yet, we hadn't talked to Grayson or Linda about staying on. Both had been showing up each day and getting on with things, but I knew that I needed to talk to them. We did decide that we would pursue our idea of hiring a server for breakfast—a person who could also help with washing up. Neither Doris nor I thought that Linda would be appropriate in that role. Her lack of teeth, cough, and permanent aroma of cigarette smoke was not the image that we wanted to portray. Linda was certainly pleasant enough in what little interaction we had had since moving here, but better in a behind the scenes role than as leading lady.

Doris said that she would get back with Mandy as soon as she could to see if she had thoughts on who might be interested in our morning job, but fate had a way of preempting that. Elsie, Mandy's mother, showed up at the door late morning.

"You want help," Elsie announced. "I'm here."

Elsie was not a tall woman; actually, she was quite short and tending to the plumpish side. Also, she was well into her seventies—maybe even close to eighty years old. This, too, wasn't the image that I wanted, but she was nice and she had experience.

"What about your work with Mandy?" I asked.

"She doesn't need me anymore," Elsie replied. "Her business is established now. Besides, I am my own woman."

I was still dithering and trying to sort it out in my mind when Doris joined the conversation. "Elsie, we would love to have the help. Why don't you and Derick discuss hours and salary, and when you can start."

As we had not talked about it, I hadn't shared with Doris that the person that I saw in the role of breakfast server was probably a sweet young thing with a bright smile, enthusiastic about everything, even a little flirty, and loaded with energy. Maybe Doris already knew what I had in mind. Maybe this is why we were getting Elsie.

"Elsie, can you be here at seven o'clock each morning?" I asked.

"No problem."

"Is eight dollars an hour acceptable?"

"Make it ten, and cash—no paperwork."

Elsie must know that the waitresses at Mandy's make a lot less per hour than that, but they could expect tips, and it wasn't the norm to tip your server at a bed and breakfast. I wanted to say, "Let me consider it," but I realized that I had not only Elsie to deal with but also Doris lurking in the background with her agenda. I could earn some brownie points by taking her on.

"It's a deal," I said. "When can you start?"

"Next Saturday if that's okay with you. I have some things to get sorted out."

Next Saturday was just right. We weren't overly busy until then, and Alec was still around "helping." This would give me a chance to be nice but gently move him on his way.

"Next Saturday is just right," I said. "Let's go and tell Doris."

Doris was happy, and I left them to talk about what clothes to wear and all of those other things in which I had no input—hair up, hair down, lipstick, eye make up, and the like.

That evening, we went to Mandy's for dinner. Interestingly, Elsie wasn't there. Mandy came over to talk to us, and we told her about her mother coming to work with us at the inn. We thought that Mandy would be pleased about her mom, so we were surprised when she said, "I know. I wish that I had had a chance to warn you."

"Warn us about what?"

"My mother," she said.

"Have we made a mistake?" I asked Mandy.

"No, not really. Actually, Mother will probably help you as you are getting started. Just don't think of her as ever being a long-time employee. She really doesn't need to work. She usually gets bored quickly, and when she does, she moves on. She's moved on from helping me."

"Okay Mandy, whatever you say," I told her. "As long as we haven't upset you, we're good with it."

"I'm good with it, too," Mandy replied.

Our new system at breakfast seemed to be working well, at least from my perspective. When guests checked in, I asked them what beverage they wanted with their breakfast. Regular coffee, decaf, or hot tea—we could just about accommodate everything. I also asked them what time they would like their breakfast and tried to give only two choices: 8:30 AM or 9:00 AM. At breakfast, I would welcome them into the dining room, tell them about the sideboard, and encourage them to help themselves whenever they wished. I showed them where the coffee was, mentioning that they could get refills as often as they wanted. I had already chopped fresh fruit into bite-sized pieces and mixed them around in a large bowl, so it was then just a matter of putting a couple of large tablespoons of fruit into a crystal goblet and bringing that to the table. As I served the fruit, I would tell them about the entrée of the day; ask their preference of bacon, sausage, etc.; and ask how they wanted their eggs prepared. I took this information back to the kitchen and helped Doris prepare and plate the meals. Alec was actually a great help. At times, he did tend to spend too much time talking to the guests when getting the information, but having him busy in the dining room meant that I could spend more time in the kitchen. It was all coming together.

One evening, a couple who had stayed at the inn many times stopped by as they were passing through. The four of us immediately bonded, and on this occasion, I was the one to suggest a glass of wine, which they accepted. We talked about the changes that we had already put in place, future intentions, and plans for running the inn. They were very encouraging. In time, the conversation turned to Catherine and Miles, and it turned out that this couple's history of staying at the inn went way back to Catherine's first husband, whom they had loved. They had no such love for Miles, but no sooner had they started to relax and tell us more than the front doorbell rang.

Catherine and Miles were at the door. They had come to say goodbye, as they were off to Florida first thing the next morning. Of course, everybody knew each other, and the conversation was initially lively and friendly. I opened a new bottle, and the seven of us—Alec had joined in—sat and talked in the parlor.

"Just a few little changes were all that you said you were going to make, Derick," Catherine said to me. "The place looks completely different."

"It's not too different," I said. "All the basics are still in place. We've really just moved furniture around."

Catherine smiled. She knew that it was our inn now, and we could do whatever we liked with it. Miles, however, suddenly turned red-faced and said, "The guests won't like it."

"But we do," the regular couple said to Miles.

"You should never have had Catherine see the inn like this," Miles went on. "It was her baby and her dream, and you've changed it all around."

"Miles," I protested, "you are the ones who just showed up on the doorstep unannounced. I didn't invite you here to see the changes we've made."

Doris was much more understanding. She glared at both Miles and me and said, "Stop it now, both of you. Catherine, is this upsetting you?"

"No, not the changes," Catherine replied. "Change is necessary, and most of them were needed. Now it's your taste, not mine. What upsets me is—" Then she lost it and burst into tears.

"Oh Catherine," we all exclaimed.

"Leave her to me, leave her to me," Miles commanded. "Catherine, leave these people and the shambles that they've created. We have just got to get out of here."

Catherine smiled at us as she continued to sob. "I'm sorry. I have to remember that it was getting too much, but I will miss it." None of us knew what to do or how to console her.

"Do come along, Catherine." Miles was now standing by the front door.

Still sobbing, she gave us all a hug, wished us well, and full of tears and sobs, put on her coat and left.

"That poor woman," I said. "Is it our fault that we bought the inn?"

"Nonsense," said our new friends. "It's the thought of her next few years living in Florida with Miles that's worrying her. Keep her in mind and one day, when you are ready to move on, contact her. You never know, but it is more than likely she will have dumped Mr. Wonderful and be ready to move back."

In a while, our new friends went to bed. We told Alec about Elsie and thanked him for his help. We said that we didn't want to keep him from his wife and life in Columbus. I think that he would have been quite happy to have called up there to say that he was jumping ship and remaining in Kentucky. But he didn't, and on Friday he packed, said goodbye, and reminded us that he could be back to help whenever we needed him.

Saturday we were nearly full—six tables would be needed at breakfast time. We were glad that Elsie was coming to help, and sure enough, she showed up right on time fired up, ready to help. I explained how we had arranged things and how we saw things working. Generally, she approved. She especially liked the sideboard and wanted to start baking for us as long as we paid for the ingredients and her time. She wanted us to number the tables, telling us that this was the way restaurants do it to keep organized. She wanted to be able to come into the kitchen and say, "Table five, scrambled and bacon; table six, ham and fried." I could see that this was a good idea but thought that we didn't have enough tables to go to this amount of trouble. As well sometimes, we had to combine tables if a group of guests wanted to sit together. Elsie accepted my argument, but maybe I made a mistake because what she started to do was describe people sitting at the table as her identifier when she came into the kitchen with the order. Elsie didn't believe in writing anything down.

She should have described the table by its location: "Right corner table, scrambled and sausage," or "Small center table, poached no meat." But she didn't.

"Green dress wants her eggs scrambled. Iowa wants extra bacon."

"Don't offer them extra bacon," I told her. "We'll be making no profits if we do that."

"I didn't offer it," she replied, "he asked for it." Then she added, "Big ears wants his breakfast in a hurry; he's late."

I noticed an older gentleman, who did have remarkably big ears, standing behind her waiting to come into the kitchen.

"Big ears here," he said. "I'm sorry. I thought that you were on Central time. I'm very late. Can you fix something simple quickly?"

"No worries," I told him.

He gave a glance towards Elsie. "All the better to hear you with, my dear."

We persevered with our policy of giving people choices at breakfast, but I was rapidly coming to the conclusion that my idea was maybe not a good one. It was very demanding on the cook, and although having Elsie meant that I could spend more time helping in the kitchen, it was still too much.

Most mornings, I would be the first one to get out of bed, shave, shower, dress, then prepare the dining room for breakfast. While I was involved in the dining room preparation, Doris would shower and dress, then move into the kitchen to start cooking. This didn't always work too well because Doris sometimes needed more time, so she started to be the first riser and I would make coffee and do what I could until the bathroom became free.

Our bedroom was on the ground floor and consisted of a large central room for the bed and furniture. Off this main room was the bathroom, and through another door, a walk-in closet. My habit after showering was to leave the bathroom without dressing, walk back into the main room, and go straight to the walk-in closet, where I got dressed. I didn't know that Elsie had started using our walk-in closet as a place to store her outer clothes and purse while she was at work.

It had to happen. My turn to be repaid for the window cleaner. One morning, I didn't get into the bathroom as early as I normally did. I shaved, showered, dried off, and skipped naked as a jaybird from the bathroom into the bedroom on my way to the closet. Skipping along, happy as could be, I suddenly became aware of a presence. Sure enough, I came face-to-face with Elsie, who had just put her coat and purse into our closet. Not that Elsie spent much time looking at my face. I was totally embarrassed, and I just froze. It took a moment for me to come to and realize that here I was, standing full frontal nudity in front of a nearly eighty-year-old woman who was gazing at my willy.

"Elsie," I called out, "what's going on? Why are you here?"

She slowly raised her eyes, looked at me straight in the face, and with a wry smile on her lips, said, "Well, we're family now. Water must have been on the cold side I'm guessing."

Oh God, the embarrassment. I dove into the closet and scrambled to put on some underpants. Elsie left, but the damage had been done.

By the time I found my way into the kitchen, Doris was well into breaking eggs and mixing in the sour cream she uses for scrambling.

"I hear that you have taken to flashing older ladies," she said, without looking up.

"Doris, what happened here?" I protested. "Why do we allow staff into our private quarters?"

"She has to leave her purse somewhere, you know," Doris went on. "You should cover yourself when you walk around the house."

"I was in our private bathroom on my way to our private bedroom to what I thought was our private closet."

"It's no big deal. Elsie has been around the block a few times, believe me. She's seen more than one or two in her lifetime." And with that, Elsie came into the kitchen.

"Good morning, Derick," she said. "Decided to get dressed then, have you?"

It didn't deserve an answer. I just glared at both of them and got about doing what I had to do to get ready for breakfast.

As time passed, it became obvious that one of Elsie's biggest problems was short-term memory loss. She had often forgotten what guests had ordered in the dining room by the time she got back into the kitchen, and she still refused to write anything down. I could cover if I sensed that Elsie was unsure by going out into the dining room and confirming what was ordered. I also did more and more of the ordering myself.

One morning, a pair of younger guests showed up very late. They still had sleep in their eyes when they sat down. Elsie took their order while I was busy clearing up other tables. The food was prepared, and Elsie brought out their plates, setting them in front of the still sleepy young couple. Somehow, the combinations on the plates were wrong.

"I asked for bacon and she asked for sausage," the young man said, "and neither of us wanted fried eggs. We asked for scrambled."

"Oh, you're family, you'll sort it out," Elsie replied, and she left them there to get on with it. I could tell that they really didn't care much. They were much more interested in each other than their breakfast, so I left them alone, too. However, there was Elsie with the "family" thing again. I was a little embarrassed at the thought of it.

At times, I am my own worst enemy, and I know that I should have just forgotten about what happened at breakfast, but there we were in the kitchen later talking about the guests. We often did that. We were late because of the sleepy couple, and for some reason, Linda was early.

I was putting on a show. "So everything on the plates was wrong, and Elsie says to them, 'You're family, you'll sort it out.'"

I wasn't trying to embarrass Elsie; I was trying to make folks laugh, which they did. However, Elsie decided to take it one step further.

"Remember Derick, you're family, you know." She mimicked herself, and with that she stared at my crotch.

I was taken aback and didn't know whether I should say anything or just ignore it. Linda, who misses very little, noticed what Elsie had done, and after an initial puzzled look, a smile appeared on her face. Who knows what she thought. Anyhow, from that day on, every now and then, Linda would look at my crotch and say, "Ha ha ha, family, eh."

Why hadn't I just let it go after that breakfast? There was no good reason to have brought it up.

The Elsie period in our lives was coming to a natural end. Elsie was tiring of what she was doing, and financially she didn't have to do it. We weren't happy either with the way we were serving breakfast, so changes had to be made. It all happened very amicably and quickly. One late afternoon, after we had checked in all the guests staying that night, Doris and I had just sat down for our evening cocktails when we heard somebody tapping on the door to the Garden room that we now had taken over as ours.

I thought that it was one of the guests asking for something, it often was, but it turned out to be Elsie. She wanted to talk to us.

"I'm moving to Arizona."

"Okay, Elsie, that's nice. When do you plan to leave?"

"I wanted to leave this afternoon but decided to wait until tomorrow. You don't need me tomorrow morning, do you?"

"No, we can get by," I said. "Is there anything wrong? Have we done something to upset you?"

"Gracious no. It's my time to move on."

"Is there anything that we need to do or anything that we can help with?"

"Here is my final timesheet."

"I'll go and write a check."

When I returned, Elsie and Doris were hugging goodbye and wishing each other well. I smiled and waited my turn for a hug, but I had to wait while Elsie got in one last dig.

"Maybe if you showered in warmer water."

"What? Oh."

"Apart from that, you're really all right for an older Englishman."

"I'll never forget you, Elsie."

"That's what they all say." And with that, she was gone.

After Elsie, we changed the way we served breakfast. One thing that I had to do was spend more time in the kitchen helping Doris. Ideally, we would find somebody who could help me and give Doris a day off every now and then. We also decided to get rid of the ridiculous menu idea. We would serve one entrée each day, and that would come complete with either bacon, sausage, or ham, our choice, and one variety of egg preparation. Some days we would have a meatless entrée, and other days we would introduce our guests to a hearty British breakfast—not the full Monty, with black pudding and tripe, but something halfway there, including fried bread and baked beans. We would look around for a replacement for Elsie, but kitchen help would be the priority.

The days passed, and we were getting more and more confident in our ability to run the inn. We had had no major mishaps, reservations were being made, and guests kept coming. The weather was getting warmer, and even though he had been coming in most days, I decided that it was time to find out exactly what it was that Grayson and his little rubber hammer did around the inn.

He would arrive each morning wearing street clothes and spend the first fifteen minutes changing into his outfit de jour. He had so many different outfits it became a little game between Doris and me to name them and then try to outguess him on what he would be wearing on a given day. For inside work, he would don a lighter weight jumpsuit that had his name embroidered over his top left breast pocket. He had a variety of hats, usually of the baseball variety, that went along with this outfit. Outside work, and probably because it was still a little cold, involved a much heavier overall suit, and hats with flaps. He changed clothes upon arrival each morning, then would find us. Usually, we'd be in the kitchen, and he would ask what needed doing that day.

Why he asked what we wanted confused us. Our usual response was, "Whatever you would normally do," and often he would tell us what he planned Sometimes we had a particular project in mind, but no matter what we said, or what he said, he would go off and work on something completely different.

Although more confident, we were still trying to find our way around the general running of the inn to be too concerned, and Catherine had told us that Grayson was completely trustworthy and honest.

If I did ask questions, his usual response was, "What to say, what to say, what to say," and then nothing. However, with the warmer weather and being a keen gardener myself, I thought that I would devote more time to finding out what was going on. Grayson had told us that he had a degree in horticulture; I was looking forward to finding out more and getting outrageously creative, with his professional help.

"What can we expect from the front flower beds?" I asked.

"Too much shade."

"Well, in the spring, before there are leaves on the trees, are there tulips or daffodils?"

"Nothing that I've ever seen."

"It's too late for this spring, but maybe we can plant something for next year," I stated.

"I sow seeds and transplant from other parts of the yard."

I wasn't getting anywhere with the front garden, so I decided to ask him about the back.

"How about the cottage garden? What usually grows out there?"

"What to say, what to say, what to say. It moves, reseeds itself every year, we have no idea what comes up. Sometimes we get exotics from around the bird feeder."

"Exotics?"

"Don't know what else to call them."

I was thinking that weeds might be a good description, but he was the expert, and I was prepared to be educated. Gardens don't always have to be pretty maids all in a row.

"Grayson, I've been thinking about composting. We have a lot of eggshells and fruit peelings, as well as scraps. We could compost them. It would be good for the environment and provide us with a nice, healthy supply of fertilizer. What do you think?"

"Would this involve me?"

"Well, yes."

"Then let me think about it."

Damn it, I thought, *we're not on the same page here. I'll just order a compost tub and tell him to get on with it.*

Later, when I told Doris, she thought that Grayson had just had his own way with the garden for a few years, probably as long as he had worked at the inn.

"Miles had no interest," she said. "All that he was concerned about was that he didn't have to do the work. It was too much for Catherine. She was busy with the day-to-day running of the inn, so Grayson took no orders and got on with what he thought needed doing. Why don't you leave him to it for the first year to see what happens? Anyway, I need your help."

"What to say, what to say, what to say," I mimicked.

"Don't be unkind, Derick!"

"I'm not, I don't think. If the plumbing goes wrong, we call the plumber. If the heating goes wrong, then it's the heating company, and the garden takes care of itself. What exactly is it that he does around here? I've never seen him help Linda with any of the housework. For instance, I want the floors polished. Will he do that?"

"Ask him."

The next morning, after the usual routine of asking what we wanted done, I broached the subject of polishing the floors.

"You shouldn't put polish down on these floors," Grayson informed me.

"Why not?"

"It'll build up."

"I sort of thought that the polish would protect the floor and has the added advantage of looking nice and making them shine," I said.

"No," Grayson answered, shaking his head. "It would just build up and not be good at all. Worst thing, in fact, that you could do is polish the floors in this house."

Our horticultural expert was also apparently an expert in preservation of old houses; however, I was becoming suspicious of his credentials.

I went to the computer, Googled "composting," and found several sites where one could order equipment. At one time in the past, I had thought about involving Grayson in the selection process of our new Primrose Inn composting enterprise, but I was no longer in that frame of mind. I made a selection, pressed "confirm order," and thought to myself, *Grayson has just got to find out who the boss is around here.*

A few days later, the UPS truck pulled up the driveway and delivered an enormous box. Grayson noticed but busied himself elsewhere as I signed off on the paperwork.

"It's here, Grayson," I called out.

"What's here?"

"The composting system."

"You didn't think to ask my advice?" Grayson said. "You know that I have a degree in horticulture."

"I just got a good deal," I told him. "Now it needs putting together."

"What to say. What to say. What to say. I suppose that you want me to help?"

I shook my head. "No, I want you to do it. If you find that you need help, ask, and I'll lend you a hand."

Grayson was speechless. He just stared at me with wide-open eyes. I had been thinking for some time that he thought he was the man in charge, and we were all there for his convenience. You didn't speak to the man in charge this way. However, I sensed that he was also intrigued about the composting system, so off he went to pick up his rubber hammer, and I left him to it.

I must admit, he did an excellent job. He put all the parts together and built a base at the far end of the garden, far enough away so that any smells that might come from the system would not creep into the house. He set the system on its base, then came to find me.

I was thrilled and told him so. I thought I might have been too rough on him. Perhaps if I just left him alone, he'd be just fine.

Later, I overheard him telling Linda that the composting was all his idea. He had originally wanted Miles to buy a system but had to wait until we bought the inn before he got his way. He had selected it and built it, and she was going to have to feed the scraps to it.

The kitchen help problem resolved itself in a most unusual way. With the warmer weather, we were worrying about bugs and spiders. Doris had convinced herself that they were lurking in all the dark spaces of this one-hundred-eighty-year-old house, waiting to come to life in the spring and make her miserable. Doris hates creepy crawlies. We called a local extermination company—the one who advertised as being environmentally friendly—and arranged for a treatment.

With great foresight, the young man who was coming to spray suggested that he not come at a time when we were serving food; instead, he would show up at our least busy time of day for guest activities. He showed up late morning after the previous night's guests had checked out and the new set had not yet arrived. We were also fortunate in that those who were staying over had gone off for their day's activities.

Doris and I were sitting on kitchen stools drinking a late cup of coffee. Linda was cleaning guest rooms, and Grayson had gone off in a huff when we told him that an exterminator was coming. He had said that I could do the same job with a spay can or two.

"You mean you would spray everywhere if I bought the cans?" I asked.

"Not me," he replied. "I don't have a license to use chemicals. You would do it. I would advise where best to spray."

"I don't have a license either, Grayson."

"You don't need one if you own the place."

"Well, I'm sure that the exterminator has a license, and he's on his way." That ended the conversation, and Grayson went about his business.

A brightly painted truck stole its way up the drive, and a short young man, face full of smiles, hopped out and made his way to the front door.

"I'm Gary Wallace," he announced, without need because he had a large badge on his lapel with his name on it.

"Pleased to meet you, Gary." I put out my hand, which he took and gave me a shake.

"I'm sorry, but we don't know when the house was last treated," I said. "Is there anything that you need to know?"

"No, I'll just get on with it and spray everywhere where I think there could be a problem," he said. "Can I get into the basement and attic?"

"Both have easy access," I replied. "I'll help you if you get lost or confused."

"I spend my life lost and confused," Gary said, still smiling.

I laughed. "Must be the chemicals," I said. "By the way, do you have a license?"

"You actually don't need one for the chemicals that we use. You do for the chemicals that make you lost and confused, and we don't use them except in a major infestation. I'll let you know how I make out and what I find."

He went off shuffling all around the house while Doris and I returned to our coffee and planning future breakfasts.

A little while later, we heard a voice calling us.

"I think that I'm just about through. Do you have a minute?" Gary said.

"Sure we do," I replied, and the three of us sat around the island in the kitchen.

"I honestly can't find anything that looks like it will pose a major problem," Gary said. "I've sprayed everywhere for an early spring treatment. You have purchased our 'Gold' service, so if anything bothers you between now and when I'm scheduled to return, just give us a call and I'll be right back. By the way, the house isn't haunted is it? We don't spray for ghosts."

"The house isn't haunted," I told Gary.

"Okay," he replied. "But you know, there is a strange looking guy in a funny hat who I noticed staring at me every now and then. He didn't say anything and just disappeared whenever I looked at him."

I smiled. "Oh, that was probably Grayson. He's not a ghost."

"Well, I didn't think that he was, but he sure looks strange. Hey, can I ask you another question?"

"Ask away."

"This exterminator gig of mine is only a fill-in for me; I'm actually going to culinary school part-time, training to become a chef. My wife and I dream about owning a bed and breakfast one day. Do you ever need help in the kitchen? I'd work for just the experience."

"You don't look old enough to be married," I said, but Doris interrupted me.

"What experience do you have?" she asked.

"None," Gary told her. "That is why I'll work for free to get some."

"Do you have any references?" Doris asked.

"Well, there is the school—you could call them. But the only breakfast experience I've had is McDonald's, and I'm sure that what you do here is different from what they do there."

"Gary, truth be known, I kind of like the breakfasts that they do at McDonald's."

"Oh, so do I, and I wasn't putting them down. I'm giving you the wrong impression, I'm sorry; I just thought that this would be an opportunity for me to get a little experience."

Doris smiled. "Gary, we'll think about it and give you a call," she said.

"Thank you, Mrs. Anderson." He smiled at her in return and got to his feet. "I'll look forward to hearing from you." With that, he was off.

I actually thought very little about Gary after he left. I suppose I was too consumed with the $105 I had spent when I could have gotten away with $20.00 with some cooperation from Grayson. Doris, on the other hand, did not let the grass grow under her feet. She telephoned Gary's school and spoke to several people about him.

That evening over cocktails, Doris told me about her telephone calls and informed me that everybody had spoken very highly of Gary. He was, apparently, quite the star pupil and popular with everybody.

"Do you want to give him a try?" I asked.

"What I want is for him to come out on our next busy morning and help. If we get a good feeling from that, I want you to offer him a job for Sunday mornings. And, by the way, we are not going to let him work for us for nothing."

"Okay, Dolly." I picked up the telephone and dialed. "Hello, Gary?"

"Yes, this is Gary."

"Gary, Derick Anderson. I want to follow up with your suggestion about coming out here and getting some commercial experience. When would be a good morning for you to sit in on our operation here?"

"Day after tomorrow works for me."

I checked our reservations on the computer and said, "We're less than half full the day after tomorrow, but that should work. We're only trying to get to know each other after all."

"What time do you want me?"

I looked at Doris and she mouthed "eight o'clock."

"Will eight o'clock be all right?" I asked.

"Sure it will," he replied. "I would have thought that you started much earlier than that. I'll see you then."

* * *

Gary actually arrived early. He explained that the exterminator truck was his only wheels, but he didn't want to park it in our drive because it might give the wrong impression. This was very thoughtful of him. He had come early to find somewhere close to park, and as there was a public lot just down the street from us, it was easy for him to pull in there and have just a short jog up the hill to the inn. He was professionally attired in his school chef jacket and pants. He'd also brought his own knives.

"What can I do?" he asked.

"Just look for now," I said. "I'm sure that you will find lots of things that we do wrong, but at least you'll become familiar with what we are trying to achieve here."

Our breakfast that morning was a French toast that Doris had prepared earlier that just needed warming up. It was served with bacon and scrambled eggs. I chopped fruit and grilled bacon, Doris scrambled eggs, and it all came together on the plate.

"Anything here that you can't handle?" I asked Gary.

"No, but I can't do it all by myself."

"That's not expected," I told him.

I was much taken with Gary and wanted to get him started, but I needed Doris's okay. I tried to catch her attention, which took some doing. When she figured out what I was signaling, she nodded enthusiastically, so I said to Gary, "Let's talk."

The three of us sat around the kitchen island.

"Gary, we would like you to come and help here. How are we going to make it work? Our idea is for you to come every Sunday morning and occasionally on other mornings if we have a crowd."

"I think that would work." Gary responded with full-on enthusiasm. "Am I at liberty to create my own dishes?"

I nodded. "Absolutely you are."

"How about purchasing ingredients?"

"If you trust us, you could e-mail or fax us a shopping list in advance of your visit, and we'll have everything ready for you."

"That'll work."

I went on. "I'll email you mid-week with the approximate number, and you email back what you want on hand. Will that be okay?"

"That works, too."

"We don't want you to work for nothing," Doris added. "Derick insists that we pay you."

I was a little taken aback, but Doris was right—only now I had to come up with a number.

"If you insist, $20 will cover me; I'm only doing it for experience."

"Derick had suggested $40," Doris said, "so let's start with Derick's number, shall we?"

"Fabulous," Gary replied. "See you next Sunday."

Gary was one of the best things that happened to us as we embarked on our careers as innkeepers. It meant that Doris had a day off, of which she took full advantage. I still chopped the fruit and prepared the bacon when needed, but Gary did everything else. He did *almost* everything else, but he was never one to do much with washing up. His meals were fabulous, creative, and delicious. He got on with everybody. I am still humbled by the way he tolerated Grayson and the way that Grayson took to him.

We exchanged our emails during the week and had everything ready for him each Sunday morning. Sometimes I would hear him walk through the backyard and open the door, other times I just awoke to great aromas wafting out of the kitchen. Doris enjoyed sleeping in late and letting him get on with it, but she did like to sneak in near the end of the breakfast serving, take Gary by the hand into the dining room, and announce to everybody that this young man was the one responsible for their morning meal. He often got applause and blushed every time.

It couldn't last. Gary was far too talented and ambitious. Even before graduation, offers were coming in and we were contacted for references. He never let us down. He was always a delight, and we learned a lot from our young chef.

CHAPTER 9

Being an Innkeeper

There was a popular British TV show called *Fawlty Towers*. The writer who also played the main character, Basil Fawlty, was John Cleese, and it was set in a small hotel in Torquay. There were very few episodes made of the show, and true enthusiasts probably know most of the scripts by heart. I've always loved that television program but never thought that I would one day live the life of Basil Fawlty—well, almost.

Now that we are innkeepers, it is apparent to us that *Fawlty Towers* was much more of a documentary or reality show than a comedy. Those sorts of situations really *do* exist, and nowadays, instead of laughing at Basil, I empathize completely and maybe become a little like him. Basil had delusions of grandeur, the go-to man in all situations, but was unfortunately inept in handing his guests or his staff or the situations in which he found himself—all with humorous outcomes.

As Basil would have done, I have mistakenly served bacon to a professed vegetarian. I realized my mistake when I got back into the kitchen, dashed back out into the dining room, only to find that the bacon had disappeared.

"I'm sorry," I said. "I can't read my own notes. It clearly says that you are vegetarian, and I apologize about the bacon on your plate."

"Bacon, what bacon?"

Well, it was gone, but I was sure that I had put it there so was then even more confused.

"Sorry about being sorry then," I mumbled, and exited back into the kitchen.

Doris didn't take too much notice. She actually became a little irritated when I started to count the remaining bacon slices. My count showed that I was missing two; I must have put them on that plate.

"Just get on with it," Doris told me. "Don't just stand there counting bacon slices; there has to be other things for you to do."

Later in the morning, when I was checking out an older couple who had been at breakfast at the same time as my bacon faux pas, the woman whispered to me, "She ate it."

"Who ate what?" I asked.

"That young woman, the one who said that there wasn't any bacon on her plate. I saw her eyes light up when you put the plate down, and she finished off that bacon quicker than a wink."

"Now that makes me feel a little better," I told the woman. "I hope that I haven't upset anybody."

"Most vegetarians fancy a little bacon now and then, especially if they can smell it when they come down for breakfast. So you haven't upset her. You've probably made her day; she got her bacon and still thinks that she is a vegetarian."

I can also be a little quick to clear up. I don't want folks to sit in front of an empty plate, and if they can't finish their meal, I certainly don't want them to have to stare at what they didn't want.

One of our regulars, Patsy, usually comes by herself. Patsy comes when there is any kind of horse show going on in the area. She is an avid fan of all things horse and can name family trees of famous horses, which horse won which race, and who are the champion show jumpers. One early stay, she was alone and I had set up a table for her by herself. This didn't always work with Patsy because she was gregarious and other guests loved her knowledge of horses. I would sometimes find that Patsy had moved her table setting to another table and was entertaining whomever it was sitting there. On this occasion, after I served her meal—and it should be noted that Patsy usually has an excellent appetite—I was cruising the dining room and saw that Patsy's table was deserted and her food only half-eaten. I looked around for her, but she was nowhere to be seen. Not wanting to leave the half-eaten breakfast, I whisked the plate up and took it into the kitchen. Later in the day, after Patsy had been out to whatever event she was in town for and was now back at the inn getting ready for her evening, I asked her about it.

"Was there anything wrong with breakfast this morning, Patsy? We don't want you to have anything that you don't want."

"No, nothing wrong with the food," she said, shaking her head. "Why have you put me on a diet? Am I looking too fat these days?"

"You're not fat, Patsy. What are you talking about?"

"I had a cell phone call during breakfast and didn't want to disturb your other guests, so I went out onto the porch. When I came back, my breakfast had been taken away. Why did you do that?"

Now it all fell into place, and I realized what an idiot I'd been.

"Oh Patsy, that wasn't me, it was some guy called Basil Fawlty."

"Who?"

"I'm sorry." I shook my head. "It won't happen again."

There really isn't anything funnier than people and the way that we interact with each other. Doris really liked our guests but seemed to be adopting an attitude that they were coming to the inn for the sole purpose of entertaining her. She began to call them clowns.

"How many clowns do we have for breakfast tomorrow? Or are we expecting any clowns to check-in today?"

It was all meant in a kind way, and Doris wouldn't dream of hurting or upsetting a soul, but it could be taken wrong—so very wrong—if someone overhead her speaking that way, so I became concerned. This was complicated by Doris not really wanting to get involved with the check-in process, which she left almost completely up to me.

I also had to go to the trouble each morning of explaining who goes with whom, where they were from, and whether they had any special requests. I'd tried to make a list from our reservation software so that Doris could look up what she needed to know, but she preferred the old-fashioned way of simply asking questions.

There were the sisters Claudine and Claudette—not twins, but close in age and very similar in appearance. Claudine would start a sentence and Claudette would finish it, or visa versa, and mostly they only talked about themselves.

"Would you care for coffee?" I asked.

"Only if it's decaf," said sister one.

"Only decaf," sister two added. "She gets agitated."

"I get agitated if I have too much caffeine. My sister never gets agitated."

"I never get agitated on caffeine, but I don't drink too much coffee, any kind of coffee."

"French toast?" I asked.

"French toast makes me swell."

"She swells up with too much French toast. I don't swell up."

"No, but you get agitated."

"I get agitated if I have caffeine."

I was having a tough time keeping all this straight.

"How about orange juice?" I enquired.

"Can't do with orange juice."

"No, she can't do with orange juice; she has an acid stomach all day if she has orange juice."

"All day, and sometimes into the evening if I have orange juice. My sister can drink orange juice."

"Yes, I can drink orange juice, but my sister has to stay away from it."

"We have cranberry juice," I offered.

"Cranberry juice tastes funny in my mouth."

"Cranberry juice makes her pucker up."

"No, I don't think that it makes me pucker up."

"Cranberry juice *does* make my sister pucker up."

My head was reeling. "One orange and one cranberry then?" I thought that I had it round the right way.

One nodded and the other smiled. I found it really odd that even though they contradicted each other, they never spoke at the same time. How did they do that?

Doris went into the dining room later and I saw her, completely lost, as the sisters were talking to her; Doris's head was going back and forth as if she were watching a tennis match on fast forward. Sometimes she opened her mouth to speak, but she was beaten to it every time by one of the sisters, so back to the head thing, back and forth, back and forth.

Then there was the clock. We have a beautiful grandfather clock that stands in the parlor. When it works, there is a soothing tick-tock and gentle chime on the hour. That is when it works. The clock is temperamental. In the past, somebody—maybe a series of somebodies—have put various pieces or wood and other objects under the feet to get the correct level for the clock to be balanced, and to keep the clock happy. I'm now convinced that this clock has a personality and has feelings. The main problem is that our floors aren't flat.

The clock had stopped working, and after several times of asking Grayson to look it over and getting no action, I decided to take on the clock by myself. I was going to clean the inside and clean the outside, rearrange the balancing; I was going to fix it up.

In retrospect, I think that the clock was looking at me as I entered the parlor with my cleaning tools. Only reluctantly did the clock allow me to pry open the door, and it swayed, making creaking sounds as I went to work cleaning its inner parts. There were two heavily weighted balls attached to chains that provided energy for the mechanism. Under normal working conditions, every third day one would pull on the chains to reset the balls from low to high. The clock didn't mind the resetting; however, old grandfather most certainly wasn't at all happy with my going after them with cleaner. No sooner had I pulled the first ball toward me to work on with my cleaning rag, than grandfather attacked.

It was a slam dunk. Using his superior height and weight to his advantage, he (the clock) fell upon me. I was pinned down on the floor by this wretched, mean grandfather clock. No blood, fortunately, but plenty of pain and bruises. Worst of all, I couldn't move. Grandfather had me pinned down solidly. I called out for Doris, and I called for Linda, but neither of them heard. I was stuck.

By chance, a nice young couple from Ohio arrived early to check-in. They later said that they thought they'd walked into a scene being made for a movie. They saw furniture in disarray; they saw a grandfather clock lying on its side. Sticking out from underneath the grandfather clock was what appeared to be a man's leg. They then heard a voice coming from underneath the clock, calling out with a British accent and saying, "I say, I wonder if you could help me."

Eventually, everything was put back together. Grandfather was put upright again, but still refusing to tick. I stay away from him. He keeps me under observation. I feel him watching, and every now and then, I can almost hear him. "Touch my balls again at your peril, Mr. Fawlty."

Housekeeper Linda was becoming a challenge. As we became more and more a part of the inn, it was becoming apparent to us that just as Catherine and Miles had not been good at throwing anything away, Linda was even worse. We moved most of the furniture that we didn't want into the barn, but that was meant to be temporary. I didn't want it in the barn; it needed to be thrown away. I told Linda that she could go down there and take anything that she wanted and that we would get rid of the rest. Linda went to the barn, came back, and told us that she would like to have all of the junk furniture but that she didn't have anywhere to store it. She said she would like to come and get one piece at a time. This wasn't acceptable, but we stupidly agreed. Now the furniture that cluttered the barn, and that I wanted to get rid of, remains in the barn; however, it has changed ownership and is now no longer mine to throw away.

Linda was also still a fright to look at, especially when she neglected to put in her false teeth. She had been a smoker for many years, so she coughed and spluttered a lot, and she got quite out of breath at anything too fatiguing. Her use of the English language was beyond belief. However, she was somewhat reliable and showed up everyday so that Doris and I weren't left to clean toilets or make beds.

Every now and then, Linda would share a little of her private life with us. She had been married and had four grown children, whom she hardly ever saw. There were also grandchildren, but even she was confused about who was married to whom and exactly where the grandchildren fit into her family tree.

Her current boyfriend, "old man," apparently the one true love of her life, seemed to lead her on a very merry dance. Billy was a short, thin, wily guy who looked a bit like a distorted Willy Nelson. We have since found out that he loves his beer, as does Linda for that matter, but Billy usually has his first beer of the day with breakfast. We suspect that that beer is usually his *only* breakfast. After a breakfast of beer, the day then falls into a pattern of popping one can after another. Because of this, Billy finds it a challenge to hold a regular job, and his driving privileges were taken away a long time ago. Billy finds casual work from time to time, but nowadays this casual work is more and more going to our Mexican imports, so Billy's main source of subsidence is Linda.

It turns out that Billy has a natural affinity to be a mechanic, and it is a matter of extreme pride that he can keep the doozey running. Not long after we bought the inn, Linda asked if she and Billy could spend the night in one of our guest rooms. Apparently, Catherine and Miles had allowed that in the past at a reduced price. It was late afternoon, and Billy was waiting for Linda next to the doozey when she asked. I hadn't been introduced to Billy up to that time, so I decided to introduce myself before I made any decisions.

Billy was swaying a little, even though he was also leaning on the car; he appeared extremely unkempt, and he smelled awful. Having them spend the night or not was not a hard decision for me to make.

"Billy, I'm Derick Anderson," I said, introducing myself.

"Awrey garwy Beell," he replied.

I'm the last person to poke fun at a regional accent. I've been living with accent challenges throughout my life in America, but I couldn't even come close to understanding Billy.

"Billy, I know that you and Linda have stayed here in the past and that Catherine and Miles only charged you $100. But

I don't feel comfortable about charging you anything at all, and we can't afford to have you stay for free. I hope that you understand?"

I don't think that either Billy or Linda understood my logic. I should have probably just said "No," but they did seem to accept it. I felt awful about it myself, and awful about turning them down. However, from their reaction, it seemed that they were used to rejection. They just shrugged it off, climbed into the doozey, then creaked and groaned and smoked their way down the drive.

Doris wanted to know why I'd turned them down because the money would have covered the cost. I explained to her that in the records, from previous stays, no money actually exchanged hands. It seemed to me that it was a Miles trick to avoid paying Linda all her salary from time to time, and that he was willing to put up with them sleeping under his roof. I didn't want to play that game.

Linda was not fiscally responsible; she didn't have a bank account and was in arrears with the IRS. Catherine had set up a system whereby Linda kept a daily record of her hours for which she was paid, and from that Catherine would set aside funds for taxes, for paying her cable TV, and for insurance on the doozey. Catherine then paid those bills as they became due. Each Sunday, Catherine would ask Linda how much she needed for the following week and would write her a check. Linda usually cashed her check at the Dairy Mart. We continued the same system, as it seemed to work; however, over time, Linda would ask for more and more in her weekly check and in no time she not only owed the IRS but she also now owed us a fair amount of change as well.

Linda's relationship with Billy was deteriorating because of his drinking, although the problem was not only that Billy drank too much; the problem was also that he didn't leave enough beer for Linda when she got home. She tried to hide her beer, but their apartment was very small, and Billy knew all the nooks and crannies. Billy's friends were also getting rougher and rougher, and he delighted in acting the lord and master in front of them, commanding Linda to get them more beer as the evenings progressed and verbally abusing her.

She was late into work one morning because, as she explained, Billy had started his previous day with a bottle of whisky. He began drinking early, switched to beer, and had run out of his favorite beverage around noon—just in time for his rowdy friends to begin dropping by to see him. Linda was working at the inn at that time. He solved his dilemma by knocking on the doors of his neighbors and offering his furniture for sale at rock bottom prices. His friends acted as movers and carried the sold furniture to whomever had bought it, and the money earned from each sale was used to buy more beer. By the time Linda got home, there was Billy, surrounded by his friends, sitting on the floor of an empty room littered with beer cans. Linda said that she was upset, but at the time, she simply joined the party and did her level best to catch up to them. As there was no bed to sleep in, she tossed and turned uncomfortably on the hardwood flooring most of the night and overslept.

The start of the end of her relationship with Billy was also to do with beer and who had the upper hand. Billy was quite buzzed one afternoon when Linda got home and had somehow gotten himself into a bad mood. He was more demanding than usual, and Linda was more stubborn than she had been before. One thing led to another, more and more cans were drunk between the two of them, name calling got worse, voices were raised, then shouting and cursing began. Apparently, neither of them was prepared to back down. Eventually the police came and carted both of them off to the pokey.

Our telephone rang at about 7:30 the next morning.

"Derick, this is Linda."

"Hello, Linda."

"Can you come and get me?"

"Where are you?"

"I'm in the county lock up next to the recreational center."

"Are you in prison?"

There was a pause. "Sort of," she said. "You are going to need $168.60 to get me out of here." She hung up.

I turned to Doris. "Linda is in the county jail," I said. "I have to go and bail her out. Do you know where the county jail is?"

"Sorry, Derick," she said, shaking her head. "You're on your own."

It wasn't hard to find. I paid the fine on Linda's behalf and drove her back to her apartment where she could wash and change.

"What is it like in there?" I asked.

"Not too bad. I knew most of the other women, and the jailer is kin to me," Linda replied, "but I don't want to go back."

"You know what you have to do, don't you?" I asked.

"I love him in my own funny way," she replied.

"Well, it's nothing to do with me, but he's not good for you, Linda. The train has just stopped at a station, and you can either get off or continue down the track to nowhere."

"I'll see you later," she said. It was just past noon.

Apparently, the great romance was destined to be over, and this incident was the catalyst. Linda had to walk to the inn the next morning because, as she explained, Billy had called his son, who lived in Ohio, to bail him out. He told his boy that everything was Linda's fault, that he was destitute, that he wanted to see his family, and that he was through with life in Kentucky, where nobody cared for him. The son had immediately driven down from Ohio to rescue his dad from a life of destitution. He bailed Billy out, took him around to the apartment, yelled at Linda that she was not taking care of her "old man," packed what personal effects Billy had, and they left. Their final act was to pour half a bag of sugar into the gas tank of the doozey to prevent Linda from chasing after them.

"Funny thing," Linda said. "Billy has an arrest warrant out for him in Ohio. He could get himself locked up for a long time if they find him."

"You're better off out of it," we told her. "Do you know anybody who can fix your car?"

"Grayson," she replied. We were amazed.

I asked Grayson and he agreed to help with Linda's car as long as he was on my payroll for time spent. I agreed and drove him to Linda's apartment so that he could work on the doozey. He took a selection of tools, as well as his rubber hammer and a good supply of orange cones, which were set in place around the car.

"Do you want me to stay?" I asked him.

He was alarmed. "You're not going to leave me here alone, are you?"

"No, I'll stay, but I don't know the first thing about anything mechanical. Ask if you need help, but don't ask me for advice."

"The car is hardly worth repairing," he said.

"Well, the repair is not costing the owner anything, and it is her only means of transportation."

"Don't let anybody pass the cones," Grayson said, as he raised the hood and stared inside.

The scene did attract attention. Some young, Spanish-speaking children were intrigued. They jabbered away and giggled while Grayson worked. There were also some women who might have been there to look after the children but were letting the kids run all over the place while they stood around in a group and chatted. A school bus stopped just up the street and unloaded some older children, who joined in the crowd. The noise level increased.

A voice from behind me asked, "Are you from the city?"

"What city?" I answered.

"I mean from the city works department."
"No, we're not."
"What is it with the cones then?" he wanted to know.
"Don't ask," I told him.
"Is he a mechanic?"
"No, but he's good with motors and the like."
"What's the problem?"
"We think sugar in the gas tank."
"Billy?"
"Probably."
"Certainly, if you ask me, he's done it before."
"Do you know how to fix it?"
"I sure know better than that guy."
"Who are you?"

"Henry Thompson," the man said, extending his hand. "I sold the car to Billy for Linda. I know her and Billy, and I've fixed everything that there is to fix on the car, sometimes more than once."

I shook his hand. Now Linda showed up. "See what Billy did to my car?" she said to Henry.

"Then you two do know each other?"

"You should have known better about that man," Henry said to Linda, referring to Billy. "And who is the yahoo that you have to fix it?"

"That's Grayson. He works with me up at Primrose Inn. This is Mr. Derick," Linda said. "He owns the inn."

"If Grayson can't get it going, can you fix the car?" I asked Henry.

"Like I told you, I've fixed everything on that car at least one time before."

"Grayson," I called out. "We've got some help here if you can use it."

Grayson was getting frustrated with the growing crowd and at his apparent inability to understand the mechanics of the doozey.

"He can help," he called back, and Henry was allowed to pass the line of cones.

With the two of them working, or at least looking into the motor of the car, I asked Linda, "Do you know Henry well?"

"Oh yes," she said. "He only lives in the next building."

"He seems pleasant enough."

"He is."

Henry called over to us. "Once we get this tank off and flush it out, we're going to need some gas to start her up."

"I'll get some," I offered, actually glad for an excuse to get out of there.

"I'll come with you," Grayson said. "He knows what he's doing here, and too many cooks spoil the broth."

Grayson was in such a hurry to tag along with me that he didn't stop to gather up his cones. We took off with a five-gallon can to get some gasoline, and I must say that I was greatly amused when we got back to see that the children had taken the orange cones and had set up soccer pitch using the cones as markers. Grayson didn't see any humor in this at all. Henry was battling with the car, and we asked if he needed any extra help.

"No," he said. "I can get her done." So we left.

The next day, the doozey puffed and panted its way up the driveway. Its back seat was loaded with all the orange cones. Linda, who was driving, was full of smiles, and next to her, also all smiles, sat Henry.

The weather was getting warmer and warmer. New growth was underway in the yard, but it seemed to me that everything that was growing was a weed. I had promised myself not to be critical of our horticultural expert until I knew the whole story. Plus, Grayson had impressed us for the first time. Grayson absolutely came into his element when it came to caring for the lawn tractor. It had been stored over the winter in the barn wrapped up in old drop cloths, but now that spring was well underway, Grayson wheeled the machine out into the sunshine, surrounded it with bright orange cones, and almost lovingly tuned, cleaned, and polished all the working parts. Admittedly, he took a lot of time doing it, but he did a far better job than I have ever done with any piece of machinery I have ever owned, and I was impressed.

"Tell him," suggested Doris.

"Tell him what?"

"Tell him that he is doing a good job with the tractor," she said.

"All he has done so far is clean it. Maybe I'll mention something to him after we see how it cuts the grass," I replied.

That was a long time coming, and the grass grew and grew. In all our time living in the United States, I've never gotten used to how long Americans keep the grass on their lawns compared to how short we trim the grass in England. I know that it has to do with the climate, but still I've never gotten used to it. Perhaps this made it worse for me looking out and seeing my new lawn turn into a prairie.

"When are you going to cut the grass?" I finally asked Grayson.

"I've been checking the weather forecast, and as soon as we have a day with no rain predicated, I'll get it cut."

The weather was most certainly one of Grayson's fixations. We would sometimes find that the kitchen TV had been turned to The Weather Channel when we were not there and not turned back.

"No rain chance at all," I asked.

"No rain chance at all," he replied.

"How about cutting the grass when the chance is less than 50%?"

"Not good for the machinery to get it wet and clogged," he went on.

"Not good for the look of the yard not to have the grass trimmed," I bantered back. "The folks across the street have cut their yard two times already. Do you want me to do it? I don't mind using a riding mower."

He looked at me in horror, and it was quite obvious that the last thing in the world that he wanted was for me to touch his—of course it was mine—lawn tractor.

Timing was on my side, and the next day was sunny and dry. "No chance of rain," the weatherman said. I mentioned this to Grayson as he pulled on his lightweight overalls.

"Remember what we said yesterday? Looks like a good day for grass cutting today; what do you think?"

"I'll test the moisture in the grass and see," he responded.

Grayson had no further excuses. The weather was fine, the lawn was dry enough to be cut, so out came the tractor—and out came his complete supply of orange cones. Sections of the lawn were portioned off, and Grayson, in his "cutting the grass outfit," sat on the tractor, laboriously going up and down in each portion cutting grass.

Just by its size, the yard around the inn looks impressive—three acres of landscaping impresses. Now that the grass was being cut, things were looking up. I could see in my mind's eye patches of color and lines of pretty maids nodding in the breeze. It must surely have looked that way once because the basic flower beds and paths were all in place and had obviously been there for a long time.

It took Grayson all day to trim both the front and back lawns, but he left the paddock, as it was getting late. The tractor had five gears, but from the speed he was going, it seemed unlikely that he ever got beyond number three. Grayson worked all day, but he was slow and ponderous, and I found that to be extremely frustrating. Also, he had not bagged any of the clippings, which would normally be all right but in this case, because the grass was so long before being cut, there were a lot of ugly clippings strewn around in clumps.

"I'm going to help you tomorrow, Grayson," I told him at the end of the day. "Either I will cut the paddock while you rake up the clippings, or you cut while I rake."

"There isn't a need to rake; the clippings add moisture to the lawn," Grayson responded.

"Grayson, it looks like shit, and I want them raked up. If you don't do it, I'll ask Arturo to get some help. In the future, if we don't let the grass grow so long we can leave the clippings, but the way they are now, they will just kill everything off." I was surprising myself with my assertiveness. Grayson didn't respond.

The next day, I got to the barn before Grayson arrived. To my surprise, underneath more drop cloths, I found a grass catcher that could be attached to the tractor to gather the clippings. I pulled the tractor out, attached the catcher, and without one single orange cone in evidence, set about cutting the paddock. I was well underway by the time that Grayson arrived, but I didn't stop. I just gave a wave as I plowed up and down on the tractor. It was pretty smooth down there, and flat, so even with the grass being long I could get the tractor up to a pretty good speed and soon had a system down where I could make two or three swathes and then dump the clippings into a pile for later use as mulch.

By the time I had finished, Grayson had partitioned off a part of the front lawn with his cones and had started to rake. I simple drove past him and vacuumed up the rest of the clippings with the catcher. He was not happy with me, but at least the yard was tidy and we had the start of a nice compost heap.

"Grayson, now that we have the lawn taken care of, what comes up in the flower beds?" I asked.

"You should turn the accelerator down before you switch the engine off," he said, referring to the tractor.

"Whatever, Grayson," I replied. "Now what grows in each of the flower beds?"

"I usually put down some zinnia seeds, and we get a lot of color," Grayson said.

"You don't use bedding plants at all?" I asked.

"Miles thought that they were too expensive, and he was quite happy with the zinnias. They grow well around here, especially if we get a hot summer."

"How would you like to take a trip out to the nurseries and help pick out something different this year?"

"The zinnias work for me," Grayson said.

"Come on," I said. "Let's take the car, and you can show me where we can buy a few bedding plants."

"I have to clear up my cones," Grayson insisted.

"Be ready in five minutes," I told him.

It was a fascinating trip. I tried to involve Grayson in conversation, but he was very guarded. I persisted, and from his answers I became convinced that he didn't care a whit for Miles. He hadn't really liked Catherine's first husband either, but he thought that Catherine was the reason the sun rose each morning and set each evening. Apparently, Catherine had asked him to help us through our transition period, so even though now I was technically his boss, and certainly the source of his income, in his mind he was still working for Catherine. I don't think that Grayson liked me any more than he had the other two men who preceded me at the inn—and maybe less.

Our first stop was a large DYI store, and there were a lot of new plats full of flowers out on display.

"What grows well here?" I asked, as we picked a basket.

"Shade plants do well under the trees; maybe roses in the sunnier parts."

I was tempted to ask Grayson for the name of the university where he'd obtained his degree in horticulture but could hear Doris in my mind begging me not to be cruel.

"Is there a local nursery with an older guy working there who might be able to give us advice?"

"Perfect Plants," he responded. "It's not too far."

"Yes, we want perfect plants," I said to Grayson.

"No," he said, shaking his head, "that is the name of the nursery—Perfect Plants."

"Oh gotcha, sorry. Let's go to Perfect Plants then and see what they have to say."

We got back into the car.

"The plants will cost more money at Perfect Plants," Grayson said, as we were driving along.

"Never mind that. We're just out to get a few ideas. Let's see what's going on there."

I didn't actually see Grayson make the switch, but when we were at the DYI store, he had been wearing a baseball hat; now, when we got out of the car at Perfect Plants, he was wearing completely different head gear—one of his hats with flaps to cover the ears.

Perfect Plants was a scruffy place, but they had six or seven greenhouses full of flowers. There was a gnarly old guy in a bib overall sitting behind an ancient cash register.

"He looks like our man," I said to Grayson. "Let's go over and see what we can find out."

Grayson reluctantly tagged along.

We had hit the jackpot. "Mr. Gnarl" was a fount of information, and it turned out that many of the horse farms and landscape people used Perfect Plants and had standing orders each year for what they liked and what grew well in the area. Before Historic Primrose Inn was a bed and breakfast, it used to have an account and a standing order at Perfect Plants. If we liked, and could give him a couple of days, he would look up the old records and let us know what had been bought for our yard in the past. He mentioned most of the common names and gave us good information on new varieties. I liked the man and promised to be back in about a week to pick up enough plants to get started.

Now it was my turn to feel sorry for Grayson, as it became apparent during our conversation with Mr. Gnarl that Grayson had no idea of what to plant or even the correct pronunciation of plant names. He misheard me when I was talking to Mr. Gnarl and had asked about Canterbury Bells, one of my favorites. Grayson, when he joined in the conversation, referred to them as Canterbury Tells. Mr. Gnarl corrected him, not me.

I wanted to cheer Grayson up since I had been a bit of a shit, so I said, "With a few bedding plants and your zinnia seeds, we'll have the place looking like a royal palace."

He did not respond.

Doris and I had had many chats about Grayson. Obviously he was unhappy, and equally obvious, I wasn't happy with him. Doris was of the opinion that we should just get on with it and leave him alone. He must be doing something, she reasoned, and what would he do if he didn't work at the inn? He had been there longer than Miles, which should count for something. I countered that all I'd ever seen him do was wander around with a rubber hammer wearing different funny hats, and I didn't know one thing that he had accomplished except to clean off the lawn tractor after the winter and assemble the compost system. I suspected that he was a phony—not harmful, but delusional, and besides I really didn't like him very much. He was arrogant.

Doris agreed that she wasn't too terribly fond of Grayson either, but she had always been more compassionate than I was and was prepared to put up with it.

The situation actually resolved itself in that when Grayson saw Henry arrive with the cones in the back of the doozey, he became convinced that Henry had come to the inn to take over his job. Henry told him that he was only there to be sure that the doozey kept running, and he wanted to keep his eye on Linda for a few days—always suspicious that Billy might come back and cause trouble. Henry did do the odd job or two around the inn but said that he didn't expect payment for his services.

It turned out that Henry really had good foresight because on the second day following the doozey repair, we were all involved in our various tasks when we heard a loud wailing coming from the area around the front gate.

"Linda, Linda, I love you. Linda, I love you, baby." There stood Billy, totally disheveled, carrying an outrageously big, shocking pink balloon and a bouquet of flowers.

"Come back to me, hon. Linda, I love you."

"More of the locals," said Grayson.

"It's Billy," Linda said.

"I'll get rid of him if you'd like," said Henry.

"No, I will," I interjected. "This is my inn, and we can't have this sort of crap going on around here." I was worked up.

I marched down the driveway. Billy had not stepped onto the property; he stayed just outside the front driveway gate. I could smell him when I was still quite a way off, but I marched forward, determined to put an end to this.

"Billy, this has got to stop," I said, as soon as I was close enough for him to hear.

"I want Linda back. I love Linda."

"You and Linda can sort all that out somewhere else. I will not have you coming to the inn and making a spectacle of yourself."

I was sure that he was drunk and couldn't help feeling a little sorry for him, but I'd had it and remained determined to put an end to the situation.

Billy looked puzzled and was probably trying to work out what "making a spectacle of yourself" meant, but he must have sensed my anger and determination to put an end to the show. He dropped his bouquet of flowers to the ground and let go of the balloon, which gently floated up and tangled itself into some tree branches. Billy then turned and walked back down the hill, back to where he was staying, without another word being said. It had been easier than I anticipated getting Billy out of there.

Back in the inn, I asked Grayson to do something about the balloon tangled up in the branches of the tree and found Linda staring down the street after Billy.

"Linda," I said, "what you do, and who you see, has nothing to do with me, but you know that you are better off without him."

She stared at me for a few seconds, and I thought that I saw a nod of her head before she turned and walked away.

"Doris, what am I doing wrong here?"

Doris smiled at me. "Nothing," she said. "Billy is the great passion in Linda's life, and you seem to have put a crimp in their relationship."

"But the guy's no good. He uses her and he abuses her."

"And she loves him."

"I don't get it." I was lost.

I didn't have much time to contemplate what I'd done wrong because now here was Grayson marching down the driveway toward the trapped balloon, with several orange cones and an extension ladder.

"What's he doing?" I said to nobody in particular.

"He said that he was going to chop the branch out of the tree," Henry shared with me.

"But that branch is huge; it will take him forever to lob it off, and it will leave a big hole in the foliage. What's wrong with trying to jiggle it free with a long pole?"

"Grayson being Grayson," Henry said.

"Please go and stop him."

"No," said Henry, shaking his head. "That's your job, dude." Henry was laughing at me now.

I took off down the driveway again. "Grayson, let's try with a long pole first."

"It's too high," Grayson said.

"Then let's use a stepladder and see if we can reach it."

"I don't do free standing step ladders. I only use a ladder that I can lean against something," Grayson told me.

"Then get the stepladder, and I'll try and get it down."

"I can easily saw off the branch."

"Good God! Grayson, that branch is huge; get the ladder and a pole, please."

With Henry's help, we got a tall stepladder and the extension pole that we used for dusting our high ceilings. While Henry held onto the ladder, I climbed as high as I dared, extended the pole, and jiggled the balloon free. I also managed to tangle some strings that were hanging from the balloon to my pole so I could bring the wretched thing back to earth without it flying off into another tree.

"Good job, boss man," Henry said.

Grayson just glared.

Grayson didn't show for work the next day. Doris and I were worried but didn't call him in case he was brooding. We didn't want to aggravate the situation. We decided that we would call him the following day if he was MIA again, but that turned out not to be necessary. Grayson showed up.

"Are you okay, Grayson?" I asked.

"Not really," he replied.

"Grayson, is it us that you're not happy with?"

"Yes and no," he said. "I'm not fulfilled; I'm not a part of anything anymore. I used to be a decision maker around here, and people respected me. I was hoping that you would make

Linda report to me; after all, I have all this experience and a degree in horticulture. But you make all the decisions, so I should probably move on."

"Grayson, this is my inn," I told him. "I wrote a very large check to buy it, and I do want things done my way. I'm sorry that you feel put out. Can we help?"

"No. I've never been to Florida, and I think that I may take a trip down there and check it out. Do you know how to get to the part where Catherine moved?"

"I can easily give you directions, if that's what you want."

"It's what I want."

"When will you go?" I asked him.

"I'll clear up my stuff from around here and head out in a few days."

"Do you want me to call Catherine?"

"No, I'll just surprise them."

"Well, you're right about that, I'm sure," I said. "I'm sorry that it hasn't worked for you around here."

"Don't be," Grayson replied. "It's time for me to move on. By the way, the cones, nobody else uses them. You don't mind if I take them with me, do you? The car might break down on the drive to Florida."

CHAPTER 10

Staff and Guest Stories

Things were coming together for us in our new way of life. We had gotten the inn shaped to our way of things, clearing out a lot of the extraneous items. We had gotten over our ambitious plans of offering menus for breakfast and were back to one breakfast entrée—one day sweet, the next day savory, to keep it interesting for guests who stayed more than one night. It didn't always work out like that, but that was our plan. Gary, our young chef, was coming in at least every Sunday and sometimes on other busy days, which eased the burden on Doris a lot. I was getting more involved in food preparation, and enjoying it, which further helped Doris. Grayson was gone; Henry had taken his place.

Linda moved in with Henry. She told us that Billy's family in Ohio didn't want him up there in case he got arrested, so he'd moved back to Kentucky. She had made up her mind to call it quits with Billy, so she moved in with Henry. Billy has apparently taken up with a large African American woman, which made Linda's transition easier. She saw a lot of humor in picturing a thin, emaciated, and somewhat short white Billy standing next to an overly large black woman.

"Most foolish thing you'll ever see," she told us.

However, that didn't last long. Billy was still drinking, and his new partner wasn't putting up with it in the way that Linda had. There was also some ill feeling about the relationship from some of her friends and family. An old boss of Billy's, who was sympathetic to Billy's situation, asked Billy if he was interested in some casual work in the country. Billy said yes and was whisked away. In his new home, well outside of town, he chops wood and clears up around a farm. He has a small, broken down shack and enough money for beer, tells everybody that he's happy and has all that he wants, but we all still worry about him coming back one day.

We were meeting a lot of interesting people now that we were inn keepers, and they were not always one of the guests. One new friend, with whom we were quite taken, was a young single mother named Marla. She had a business taking people on tours of horse farms. We are often asked by our guests to arrange tours of horse farms, and Marla does an excellent job—or so we were told. We'd also been told that the horse farm people like her as well, and she can often get folks into some of the farms that don't usually allow visitors.

Marla was as cute as a button. She had a trim little figure, stood no more than five two, always had a smile, and was always cheerful. Her one distinguishing feature is very heavily beveled eyeglasses; she could see very little without them.

Marla also has a six-year-old son named Jack. Jack, too, is adorable—very polite and anxious to help out whenever he came around. Jack and I bonded in a pseudo-grandfather, grandson way, and although he would never take the place of my real grandchildren, I liked him a lot and looked forward to his visits.

Sometimes, when she couldn't make other arrangements, Marla would ask if she could leave Jack in our company when she took a group on a tour. Jack and I would get involved with projects or just hang out.

Alec continued to visit often. He would call on certain Fridays and say that he was on his way down for the weekend. He was still off the wall, but everybody liked him, and he did keep the place cheery. Alec and Marla hit it off, and of course Alec and Jack seemed just made for each other. They played ball in the paddock and had wonderful games of hide and go seek all throughout the inn. When it rained, they had an ample supply of board games to keep them busy. I loved to see them together. It seemed that by having a six-year-old to play with, Alec didn't have to behave like a six-year-old himself. Their laughter together was incredibly infectious.

Even though we were seeing a good amount of Alec, it had been a while since we saw the rest of the family, so decided on a party. We would close off the inn to guests, invite our children with their children, and their extended families, too, if they wished to come. We sent out invitations.

Everybody came, and we all had such a good time that we decided we should plan on having these get-togethers more frequently. Thanksgiving and Christmas seemed to be ideal choices.

Our main problem in running the inn now was fatigue. Whereas in our previous life it had seemed there was little to get out of bed for first thing in the morning, now we were busy until about 10:00 AM—and almost on the tick of that hour, an extreme tiredness would come over us both.

The guests were still coming at a reasonable rate—especially when the local track was open, and we also had people staying with us at the time of the Kentucky Derby in Louisville, just about one hour's drive away. Doris is hilarious during the racing season because often, guests will come down for breakfast, then return to their rooms to change into their "going to the track" outfits. Doris doesn't recognize them when they come down for the second time all dolled up.

One time, a very well dressed woman was wandering around in the library. Doris went up to her and said, "Welcome to Primrose Inn, can I help you?"

With a look of amazement, the woman said to Doris, "You served me breakfast less than an hour ago."

"Did you enjoy it?" Doris asked.

"Yes."

"I'm so glad. Have a good day at the track," Doris replied. She didn't know that I had overheard the whole encounter, and it still makes me smile.

The different seasons and different events bring completely different types of guests. One of our favorite groups is the farriers, who come in a couple of times a year for a continuing education course. They aren't too far removed from the old time blacksmiths. Most are men, most are burley, and *all* are loud, raucous, and funny. They fill the parking lot with large vans that have been adapted to each individual's needs, no two of them the same. They fill the inn with laughter trying to outdo each other with stories of animals they have shoed other than horses, and stories of horse owners who have no idea what end of the horse gets the food bag and what end gets the rake. Their day starts early compared to our usual bed and breakfast guests, often requesting breakfast at 7:00 AM. They are always on time and have excellent appetites.

Fred is one of our favorite farriers, and he comes to most of the sessions—perhaps because he is farther off the wall than the rest. He is a big man with a loud voice and a great enthusiasm for life. He is devoted to his trade and has a great love for all animals, as well as people. Fred's eyesight is deteriorating, as with everybody else's, but Fred so far has declined to wear glasses. One morning, he woke early but couldn't see his wrist watch well enough to tell the real time. He got confused by an hour and was convinced that he, and everybody else, was late. He went around the inn banging on all the doors shouting,

"Get up, get up. We're going to be late. Dr. P. hates it when class starts late."

Doris and I were awake. Doris had made it to the kitchen to get breakfast underway, and I was just finishing up in the bathroom. By the time I got to the kitchen, I found Doris doubled up with laughter.

This was not the usual way Doris starts her day. "What's up?" I asked her.

"Oh, it's Fred. He got confused about the time and has been banging on all the doors to get people up," Doris told me.

"*All* the doors?" I asked.

"All the doors," she replied.

"Even the doors of guests who have nothing to do with the course?"

"All the doors," Doris said, nodding.

"Where is he now?" I wanted to know.

"He has gone off to find the newspaper."

Sure enough, there was Fred marching around in the front yard looking for the place where the newspaper agent had thrown our morning news. He passed it a couple of times; his eyesight was getting worse. In the end, I took pity on him and gave him some direction.

"Got the group up on the early side?" I asked.

"These old eyes—you know, Dr. Patton likes everybody to be there five minutes before the start time."

"I know, Fred, but the folks who are not going to Dr. Patton's don't need to be up early, too."

"I didn't know who was in which room. So I knocked on them all," he said, laughing. "Do you think that Doris will have coffee brewed by now?"

"Probably, but are you sure that you want caffeine?"

"I love the stuff," Fred replied.

There are other instances with guests who have refused to take advantage of medical advances. Often, it is to do with hearing. Both Doris and I are going a little deaf, so we understand somewhat about the gentleman guest from Alabama, with his pretty, quiet, diminutive, and probably trophy wife. He had a loud voice—probably so that he could hear himself. He was a large man and commanded attention with appearance as much as with sound. When he checked in, he proudly told me that he was from Montgomery, Alabama. He was forceful when he spoke, and it almost sounded like a challenge. He also spoke in statements. He asked for restaurant recommendations and had to be told several times, so perhaps I should have realized then that he was hard of hearing. I just thought he was distracted and not listening to me.

Next morning, with a pretty full dining room, he walked in with his quiet, diminutive trophy wife. He marched up to the sideboard and helped himself to juice.

Were you comfortable last night? Did you sleep well?" I asked him.

"We're from Montgomery, Alabama," he replied, in his loud, assertive voice.

I said nothing, just smiled at him and went off to get something from the kitchen.

Later, as I was going from table to table topping off coffee cups, I asked, as I do, if everyone who had wanted dinner recommendations the night before had found a restaurant to their liking. I asked our southern gentleman.

"We're from Montgomery, Alabama," was the reply again, this time even louder and more assertive.

I was lost and confused and standing in the middle of the dining room with a carafe of coffee in my hand, at a loss to know what to say to the man next. It was the other guests who came to my rescue—first one table, then two, then all of them began to snicker. Some of them were looking at me with sympathy behind their smiles.

"What's wrong with him?" I heard the southern voice again. "How many times do I have to tell him that we are from Montgomery, Alabama?"

The trophy wife remained stoic throughout the encounter. She didn't crack either a smile or a frown. She knew where her bread was buttered, that one. However, people at some of the other tables began laughing out loud. Doris came out of the kitchen to find out what was going on. She glared at me and raised her eyebrows.

"What?" was all that she said.

"Just me being stupid," I told her.

I've found out that I can be extremely stupid. When there is nobody around to blame, I have to admit that I'm as batty as the people that I work with these days.

We have one couple who stay at the inn often. They are extremely rich, probably have more money than God, but they like our little cottage in that it provides them with privacy. They are also quite well known as horse owners and breeders. On one occasion, during our first summer, they were coming to stay for the second time since Doris and I bought the inn. It was hot, and Linda told me the morning of the day that they were due to arrive that the air conditioning in the cottage wasn't working. In the past, she said that Grayson had gone out there with his rubber hammer, and sometimes got it fixed. Well no more Grayson, and no more rubber hammer. I asked Henry if he had any ideas and he said, "No," not if I wanted a guarantee of a fix for the same day. I called our local air conditioning company, and even though I still had trouble making some folks in Kentucky understand what I say to them over the phone, I got an assurance that somebody who knows my air conditioning system would be out there as soon as possible with a guaranteed fix.

The day drew on, and no repairman appeared. I called again: "Don't worry, he's on his way." Still the minutes and hours passed.

The "richer than God" guests arrived. I was overly apologetic in explaining the situation to them. They were extremely gracious and nice.

"Don't worry," they said. "We have to go out for a business meeting that could go on quite late. We'll just get changed, and we're sure that it will all be fixed by the time we return."

The moment they pulled out of the driveway, the repairman arrived. He looked at the machinery, pronounced that it was nothing hard to fix, spent about fifteen minutes going back and forth between the cottage and his truck, and then told us that the problem had been put to rights.

"It's going to take about two hours to get the place cooled off," he told us as he left. It was 5:45 PM.

At 7:15 PM, even though I knew that it had not yet been a full two hours, I thought I would go and check that indeed the cottage was cooling itself off.

Perhaps I should have counted how many cars we had in the parking lot. Most of the guests were out, but not all. So the four or five cars didn't seem to be a large number to me.

To my credit, when I opened the cottage door with the pass key, I did yell out "Innkeeper." The richer than God guests had returned early from their meeting, and there they stood with looks of great surprise on their faces. You know, it doesn't matter how much money you have when you're in the middle of undressing for bed—we all look very much the same.

I was mortified. "I'm so sorry," I mumbled, as I made a hasty retreat.

Thank goodness for nice people, and these folks are amongst the best. The next morning at breakfast they were full of smiles and ready to tease me about the night before. It turns out that their dinner meeting had been interrupted by an emergency for their hosts, and it had been put off for a couple of weeks. They'd decided on an early night with pizza delivery, which they hadn't done in years, so had returned to the inn and the Cottage. When they heard a noise outside their door, they first thought that I was the delivery of their pizza, but when the door opened and I walked in, they did have some concern. Thank goodness that I called out "Innkeeper." However, it was the look of compete embarrassment on my face that made them relax.

They said that they had enjoyed a good laugh about it all when the pizza eventually arrived, by which time they were quite presentable in night robes. They did make another reservation for the night of their delayed meeting and have been back several times since.

We provide bathrobes for our guests to use when staying at the inn, but very rarely do we see them at breakfast. Most guests dress in street clothes before they come down to eat. There was once a slight variation on this rule. A group who gets together once a year and stay at different bed and breakfasts has gotten into the habit of wearing bathrobes to breakfast. Over time, they made up their own robes and had the names of all the inns where they'd stayed embroidered on the back like a t-shirt from a rock band tour. They were an older group of people, and there were eight of them, so they had taken most of our rooms.

When they checked in, they asked two things: was it all right if they served their own Bloody Mary's with breakfast, and was it all right if they wore their bathrobes. I said "Yes" to both but later received a good telling off from Doris.

"What about the other guests?" she asked. "You are prepared to allow these old fogies to come down to breakfast in bathrobes! What kind of inn will the others think we run here!" She wasn't at all happy with me.

The next morning, with some trepidation, I waited for everybody to arrive in the dining room. I had arranged the tables so that the large group would all sit together at one large table, and our other guests were spread around at separate individual tables. I had set out pitchers of Bloody Mary mix; they were bringing their own vodka. Doris was busy in the kitchen and maybe generating more clattering than usual.

Eight o'clock, soft music playing quietly in the background and the first arrivals began to drift in. None of them were from the large group, and soon all the individual tables were filled and a usual breakfast was underway. Doris kept drifting into the dining room to check on what was going on and to throw me looks that meant, "What have got yourself in for this time?"

Finally our large group arrived en mass. They were all wearing their bathrobes and talking animatedly. They filled the room with chatter and noise, found their seats around the big table, and poured Bloody Marys. I retreated to the kitchen and said to Doris that she just had to go out there and see what was going on. She looked at me with daggers but took in a breath, and off she went into the den of inequity. I followed.

Our old fogy bathrobe groupies were indeed wearing their bathrobes, but they all had on their regular clothes underneath. They were laughing and having a good time pouring Bloody Marys for the other guests and just generally enjoying themselves. Doris absorbed what was going on, and she actually accepted a Bloody Mary and joined in the fun.

"You dodged a close one there, Derick," she said to me, when we were back in the kitchen.

"What sort of inn do you think this is?" I replied sarcastically.

* * *

SEMI-RETIREMENT

Some of my favorite memories are the times when Doris tries to be especially nice to older gentlemen. Doris likes older gentlemen, and she likes them best when they are so clean that they look polished. She also likes them to be as polite as this guest was. He had finished his breakfast and was serving himself to another cup of coffee. Doris looked daggers at me because she presumed that I had missed the sweet old guy when I'd made a coffee run around the dining room. I hadn't missed the sweet old guy; he had said no to more coffee at that time, then later changed his mind. Off she went into the dining room to put things to rights. She beat the sweet older gentleman to the coffee pot and insisted that she pour, so he held out his cup for the refill. As noted, he was an older gentleman, and the poor guy was just a little shaky as he held out his cup. Doris started to pour, and the cup became a moving target. She had to chase the cup around with the pot. The inevitable happened, and the older gentleman finished up with hot coffee spilt all around his crotch and down the front of his freshly pressed trousers. With great aplomb, he totally ignored the accident, thanked Doris for his coffee, and headed back to his seat at one of the dining room tables. It was too much for me. I headed for our sitting room convulsed with laughter. I also needed to hide from Doris because I didn't want her to find me laughing.

Another time, when another of Doris's favorite people—this one was a clergyman, the Reverend Daniel—was visiting, Doris went to introduce herself at breakfast because she had missed him when he checked in the night before.

"Good morning, Reverend Daniels," she said.

"No, it's singular," he replied. Doris had said Daniels not Daniel.

"Oh, good morning, Reverend Singular then," Doris went on, with a beautiful smile on her face.

He looked at her in complete amazement.

Later, when I took his breakfast to him, I came across him kneeling on the floor instead of sitting at the table. He had dropped his napkin ring and was having trouble retrieving it. I helped him.

Back in the kitchen, after I'd returned, Doris said that she thought it was nice of me to join Reverend Singular in his morning prayers.

It was my turn to look at her in complete amazement.

Sometimes, considering the kind of background we come from and the life we lead, I do wonder about the sort of inn we run. Doris and I are very proper but tolerant of other people's ideas and moral codes, or at least we hope that we are. There is an unspoken rule in the bed and breakfast business that if anybody leaves anything at the inn, one doesn't contact them, one waits until they contact you. One never knows whether a guest wants to keep their stay private. Most folks who leave things like cell phone chargers, various items of clothing, etc., do make contact later, and you mail the left items to them. But items are sometimes left and nobody calls. We keep them for a while before we throw them away. Items of clothing that get left are the most intriguing—especially the ones that Linda calls "Fredericks of Hollywood." It has been an education for Doris and me, and sometimes we wonder if these bits and pieces are left because people actually do forget them or if they're left so that they will never be used again—much like the way The Who broke their guitars after a concert. Of course, The Who might have broken their instruments in order not to play an encore; maybe these guests ran out of time, too.

When Linda puts bathroom rugs in our upstairs washer, they have a tendency to clump up together in the spin cycle, and the washing machine will start to dance around and we hear a rhythmic thump, thump, thump as far away as downstairs. Usually when one of us hears this, we climb the stairs to the washer and take out the offending rugs. It doesn't happen often but often enough for us to know what is going on. As the thumping would most certainly bother guests staying in the adjoining room, it is almost a no thinking reaction for us—thumping means taking rugs out of the washer, especially if there are guests in the adjoining room.

We had an elderly couple check in early one afternoon. Their room was the adjoining room to the washing machine. It is an upstairs room, which meant quite a long climb; we usually try to reserve a ground floor room for elderly people, but the downstairs rooms had been taken by others. They were very nice, and I thought it due to old age that when completing the reservation form the older gentleman didn't know whether the older lady wanted coffee or tea with her breakfast. I gave them the key to their room, and off they went to climb our handsome staircase. It was a struggle for them both. Doris met them and thought that they were sweet.

"Maybe we'll be just like them when we get to be that age," she said, after they went upstairs.

We went about our business. Linda finished up and gave us the status of the rooms; this one is ready; this one still needs the lights turned on; there is a load in both washers and dryers, and a load waiting downstairs. About an hour later, Doris said that she was going upstairs to turn on lights, and I sat in our private room hoping to enjoy some live soccer from the English Premier League on Fox or ESPN.

Thump, thump, thump. *There goes the upstairs washer,* I thought, and took myself up the back stairs to stop the noise so as not to disturb the older couple staying in the adjoining room. I got there at about the same time as Doris, who had also heard the thumping and had come up the main staircase.

"I'll take the rugs out to dry on the clothesline outside," I said to Doris.

"I'll help you," she replied.

We opened the washer, and there were no rugs in there, just a load of sheets and pillow cases that were already quite dry and had obviously finished their spin cycle a while ago. We looked at each other in some amazement, and then heard the thumping start again. It was coming from the other side of the wall.

Realization hit us both at the same time and enormous grins spread across our faces.

"You know, Dolly," I said, "I, too, hope that we are just like them when we get to that age."

Doris giggled. "I think that I know where Alec gets his immaturity from."

Then there was the sweet young thing who was traveling alone on business, something to do with an audit at our local hospital. She had RN behind her name, so this indicated that she was a nurse and was quite self-assured, as most people who travel a lot tend to become. She reminded me of my old life when I spent a lot of time on the road. I showed her to her room and asked if she needed anything. She had questions about how to operate the television and how to operate the Jacuzzi, how to lock the door, and strangely she asked if she could run around naked inside her room. I was sure that she was trying to embarrass me, so I took up the challenge and said to her, "Running around in your room naked is quite acceptable as long as you call me first."

I had been back in the kitchen for about ten minutes when the telephone rang. It was the tone on the telephone system indicating an in-house call. Doris was next to the phone and could tell from the light that it was the room where the nurse had just checked in.

She didn't answer, just said to me, "It's that aggressive pharmaceutical person who you just checked in."

"Really," I replied. "Why don't we just let the answering machine take it?"

No message was left, and even though pleasant the next morning over breakfast, the aggressive pharmaceutical person hasn't ever been back.

Another morning and another nurse, as it turned out, came down to breakfast with her husband, and as I was serving them their entrée, she looked up at me and said, "I dreamed about you last night."

I was completely taken aback. My eyes opened wider and wider, and I nearly dropped the plates of food.

"Me? Nobody dreams about me!" I told her. "Not unless it's a bloody nightmare."

All this time her husband is just sitting there with a Cheshire cat grin on his face.

"But I did," she went on. "The house was on fire—not this house, but I was in there and trapped. You burst through the flames and carried me out."

I was completely lost for words. Her husband, of all people, came to my rescue.

"It happens all the time with her," he explained. "She has the most unusual and vivid dreams, and she remembers every little detail of them."

I was still stunned and couldn't speak, so I backed out of the dining room to the comparative peace of the kitchen. Doris, of course, who barely misses a trick and had heard the whole encounter said, "Dreaming about you now, are they?"

"Ah-h-h-h-h . . . " I still couldn't make any more words.

"Just don't let it go to your head."

Doris went to the couple and said, with a big grin on her face, "I heard that you dreamed about my husband last night. He'll never get over it, you know." Pretty soon, they were laughing and joking together while I was left in the kitchen feeling very left out of it.

On another occasion, we had a guest staying with us who had a very broad southern accent. It wasn't unpleasant, just difficult to understand. I had to ask him to repeat himself several times when he asked questions, but my biggest challenge was when he asked if my Wi-Fi was available. Through his southern drawl, I thought he had asked if my *wife* was available, and I didn't know how to answer him.

Perhaps my worst encounter of this sort was during a quiet time of year when Doris had taken the opportunity to visit Lower C and the grandchildren and get some time away from the inn.

We had only two guests, both women, one young and one a little older. The young one it turned out had recently broken up with her boyfriend after a number of years spent living together. She wanted time away to be by herself. The older woman was a woman of means, and she was in the area to tour horse farms. I broke one of my rules and sat them together for breakfast. After a slow start, they did break into conversation and pretty soon were jabbering away and becoming close.

They ended up spending the day together, visiting horse farms and antique shops. They were still jabbering away well into the evening. They invited me to join them for a glass of wine, and perhaps I shouldn't have, but as I was on my own, I did. Then I opened a new bottle or two.

The younger woman, who was staying in one of the upstairs rooms, announced that it was time for her to go to bed. She gathered herself together for the climb up our grand staircase. Obviously she had had a good day and was grateful to her new friend for helping her through a difficult patch in her life. Her new friend said that she, too, had had a good day. She had been helped as well by simply talking to both the young woman and, for some reason, me. We said goodnight, and the younger one left. There was still wine in the bottle, so I asked my new friend if she wanted another glass before she turned in. She was staying in a downstairs room so didn't have to climb the stairs.

"Yes," she said. "You know, I *have* had a good day, and I think that I have been of some use as well. That young woman is going through a difficult time and needed to talk."

"You've been very kind to her," I told her.

"Maybe, however, it has unsettled me."

"What do you mean?" I asked.

"Oh, she had done so much in her young life, and with plans to do and find out more. Compared to hers, my life is boring. It seems to be passing quickly, and I've not had nearly the same experiences that she has had."

I guessed that the wine might be taking over, but I felt sorry for her and didn't want her to be unhappy. She was not an unattractive woman, maybe a little on the pudgy side, but she had a kind face on top of a full figure.

"Sometimes," I told her, "maybe we all think that we have not taken every opportunity open to us." And I was going to add more, but she interrupted.

"Do you think that?" she said. "I'm glad to hear it. You know that I haven't been with a man in nearly twenty years."

This got my attention. Where was this going? What was I doing? Had I given her the wrong impression? She knew that Doris was out of town.

"You're a good looking woman," I told her. "I'm sure that you could do something about that whenever you want to."

"How about now?"

"Now?" I was startled. "There are probably unwritten rules about innkeepers and guests," I told her, "and I'm breaking them just talking to you about this, let alone drinking all this wine."

"I'm going to my room," she said, "and will leave the door ajar. It's up to you. I've told you that I'm out of practice, but that young woman today has got something stirred up in me to be with a man again." She left.

The first thing that I told myself was that it was not me that she was interested in; it was just that I was the only bloke in the house. The next thing that I thought about was whether I could get away with it. The young one upstairs was certainly more what one has in mind when considering a dalliance, but to have been asked outright by a pretty good looking woman wasn't bad. What to do? What to do? What would I do if Doris found out? And that final thought is the one that made up my mind. I'm a happily married man. Take a deep breath and go to bed—alone.

I went around the house turning the lights off and in the process had to pass a slightly open bedroom door where the older woman was staying. Eyes straight ahead, I walked past the open door.

All of this had gotten me somewhat agitated and wound up, so I decided to watch a little TV as a distraction before attempting sleep. Our private sitting room was not too far from the bedroom in question, the one with the door half open. I tuned the TV, kept the volume low, and tried to relax. It was difficult to concentrate. Maybe I should get myself a drink. But this meant passing the open door again, and perhaps she could hear me, and perhaps I really wanted to go in there.

I still couldn't relax, and now to make matters worse, there was some interference on the TV screen. The picture had become fuzzy, and there were flickering lines going across. *I have to get that drink,* I told myself. *Just walk straight past that door; forget what is in there.* After a deep breath, I headed for the bar.

The bedroom door was still half-open as I passed, and now I could hear a buzzing sound coming from in there like that from an electric toothbrush. I stopped, and thought I could also hear some low moaning and an occasional gasp, as if somebody was catching their breath. *Keep moving, Derick. Don't even try to imagine for a second of what could be going on in there. Just think that it is only a lonely woman cleaning her teeth.*

In the bar, I poured myself a big one and took it to our bedroom, where I locked the door. No ice, no water—neat booze, something that would get into my circulation quickly, work its way to wherever it goes, and calm me down. What a night this turned out to be.

There was only one guest for breakfast the next morning. The young woman, who looked refreshed and happy, asked where her new friend was, and I told her that I didn't know. The downstairs bedroom door was now wide open, and the woman who'd spent the night there was gone. On the bedside table was a little note:

Mr Anderson, I've decided to try for an earlier flight so won't be here for breakfast. Please charge my credit card for anything outstanding, and say goodbye to the young woman upstairs when she wakes.

You do find out a lot about yourself when running an inn, and you also find out wondrous things about others. There are two young couples who visit regularly; they seem very close and always appear to be having a good time. It turned out that one of the women became pregnant, but not by her husband. The father appeared to be the other man in their group. It didn't bother them a bit; they just switched their arrangement around. They still visit regularly but now each woman is with the opposite man. They are still all very close, and they still seem to have a good time.

***

After we had been in the inn for a year, the economy took a turn for the worse, and we started to notice a decline in our business. At first, this was welcome. We had bitten off more than we could chew anyway, but when we bought the place, we thought that with sufficient money coming in, we would hire staff to take care of the extra work. Gary had graduated and was immediately snapped up by a restaurant in a full-time position. I was coming along with my cooking skills, and had no complaints from the guests, so I was spending more time in the kitchen. We thought it would be better to replace Gary with a server who could also help with the washing up. Mandy helped us look and recommended a sweet young thing who worked some evenings for her in her restaurant.

Lauren was approached and accepted our offer. She didn't get much of a salary working for Mandy, but whatever she made was supplemented by tips. We offered more because we didn't expect that our guests would tip at breakfast time. We also wanted her to do more than serve tables; she was expected to help with washing the dishes and preparing the dining room for the next day.

Lauren was young and really quite a pretty young lady. She said she enjoyed not having to wear a uniform and took the opportunity to show off her good looks by turning up in very flattering outfits. She was an incredibly proficient waitress and could carry three plates of food on one arm. She was fast and flitted around the dining room making sure that everybody had everything that they wanted. She joked with the guests and was always ready with a quip about one thing or another. Plus, her local knowledge was handy when folks had questions about where to go and what to see.

Much to our great surprise, guests would leave tips. She would proudly walk into the kitchen with one dollar and five dollar bills that were then left on the counter for all to see. This didn't go over at all well with Linda. If the money was still there when she showed up, Linda would stare at it and grumble a little in her throat. Linda also expected tips, and sometimes she got them. Some guests left money on a pillow or bedside table. The fact that Linda was envious of Lauren and her tips became more and more of a problem, and we expected trouble one day.

As proficient and pleasant and quick as she was, over time, Lauren proved to be unreliable. It must be hard for a young woman in her early twenties to be up early and working most mornings, especially weekends, our busiest time, when she had been working the evening before. Lauren also enjoyed going out with her friends after the evening job, which made bedtime even later for her. We started to get phone calls five or ten minutes before she was due to arrive telling us that she was running late. Sometimes her cat was missing, and she didn't want to leave it outside. Sometimes her car was acting up—there were a lot of excuses.

It made things difficult for Doris and me because there was no backup for Lauren, and as much as we loved everything that she did when she was there, when she didn't show it was left to us again. Doris suggested that we think again about having Linda work in the dining room, but the sad truth was that no matter how nice she could be when she tried, Linda smelled like an ashtray, she had no teeth, and she had a very poor command of the language. This did not add up to what most folks want to have serving their breakfasts. She also had a very bad habit of coughing first thing in the morning and after exerting herself. It just wouldn't work. We needed a plan "B."

Of all people, it was Alec, now almost a permanent visitor of ours, who came up with a solution.

"What about Marla? She could use the money."

Alec and Marla had been seeing quite a lot of each other over the past months. They obviously liked each other's company. We weren't sure how Marla put up with Alec's wackiness, but in truth, he wasn't his usual way out whacky self around her.

"Do you think she would be interested?" we enquired.

"It's her dream to run a bed and breakfast, plus her business is off during this economic downturn—you might have noticed. Anyway, I'll be here to lend a hand as well."

"Don't you have a job to go to, Alec?" This from Doris.

"More like drudgery."

"Don't you have a wife to go to also?" This from me.

"That's getting to be more like drudgery, too."

We called Marla, and she was thrilled with the idea. She said that she would love to work the breakfast shift, with the only proviso that she could get off in time for her tours on days when she had them.

"What about Jack?" I asked.

"Well, I could take him to my mom and dad," she said. "Mom still works part-time so doesn't have to be in early every morning On those mornings when she does, I'm sure that dad could help out."

"Would you ever consider just bringing Jack with you here? He can hang out with me," I said. "I love that little chap."

"Of course I would, Derick. He loves you, too."

CHAPTER 11

Is This Worth It?

Over time, we found that inn keeping could be wearing, even though we now had a somewhat reliable staff: Linda, who cleaned; Henry, who did odd jobs and most of the yard work; Marla, who helped with breakfast; and Alec, who was Alec. We still found ourselves getting tired, almost to the point of exhaustion. Doris and I shared menu planning, shopping, bookkeeping, and we answered all the questions on both the telephone and across the Internet. We were concerned about this, especially due to the fact that our occupancy rate, because of the recession, was not what we thought it was going to be. The original calculation suggesting that we would take in about two times more than we would pay out each month had not held up. Some months, we didn't even break even, which was very disheartening. I called the bank to enquire about restructuring the debt and getting our monthly payments down, and they helped a little, but everything else costs more than it had, and the guests were not coming in the same numbers.

Other aspects of running an inn were also becoming a little wearing. Guests hardly ever showed up at the time when they said they would arrive. Back when we were shopping to buy an inn, I remember being puzzled by the negative attitude of some of the owners—particularly those guys in Georgia—when we showed up early. Early is worse than late because the room might not be ready, but late without a telephone call letting us know was equally frustrating and interfered with evening plans. Some people also failed to understand about checkout time, and that was as important as check-in—especially when a room needed to be cleaned for the next guest. Off they trot after breakfast for a walk around town or some other sightseeing adventure; some even go back to bed. We tried to accommodate everybody, but it became difficult on us, especially if we wanted to go somewhere but had to stick around to check them out. The morning was then shot, and we were required to be there in the afternoon for check-ins, so the afternoon was shot, and some check-ins were bound to be late, so the evening was shot. Then there were the excuses for canceling or not showing up at all. Some people could be incredibly creative about telling you stories of distant aunts having heart attacks in the middle of the night necessitating a drive through the wind and rain for several hours, so now they can't keep their reservation, and we won't apply our cancellation policy, will we?

My particular challenge was with the folks who just showed up and wanted to merely look at the inn. The concept that a bed and breakfast is actually your home, and folks who stay are guests, albeit paying guests, but guests nevertheless in your house where you live is lost on some people. Some just march right in without a knock on the door or a ring of the bell, wander around wherever they wish, and even wake you from an afternoon nap in front of a TV football game asking inane questions. After three years, we were getting a little jaded, and we needed a break.

But then there were the guests who had become friends, the ones we looked forward to seeing time and time again. One of our regulars recently said that when he got to within one hundred miles of the inn, he got a warm feeling that he'd soon be back to his second home. Those people, we would surely miss.

SEMI-RETIREMENT

* * *

We thought we were right in our decision to go with small, individual tables in the dining room. We could put them together for a large group when needed, but otherwise guests were not obliged to talk to one another. Sometime they did chat away, and we tried to encourage it, but other times one could hear a pin drop in the dining room, it was so quiet. Doris especially didn't like the quiet times, and she encouraged me to go out into the dining room and get a conversation started.

One memorable morning, we were quite full with one reasonably large group of six and several others in twos. The six were around a large, single table. It was deathly quiet, and Doris was not handling the silence well. Doris marched up to the group of six. "Come on, you people," she said. "Snap out of it! Let's hear some noise." It was then that she realized that they were all holding hands and bowing their heads in prayer. The other guests were keeping quiet in deference to the prayer meeting. Doris turned red, the other guests grew wide-eyed, and I collapsed in uncontrollable laughter back in the kitchen. Then the sounds of my laughter made the non-praying guests begin to giggle. One could see them heaving their shoulders. Fortunately, the giggling became infectious, and soon the religious group was laughing as well.

I accused them all of laughing in church, which made the situation worse, and they laughed even louder. Soon everybody was laughing, except poor Doris, who was awfully embarrassed and apologized profusely to everybody during and after breakfast. But no damage done. They were all nice people. No damage done either the time I carried a plate into the dining room and nearly put it into the upturned hand of another devout guest, who was in the middle of praising whatever she praised first thing in the morning. I just caught myself in time and set the plate down in front of her instead of trying to balance it on her upturned hand. The guest smiled at me in thanks, and I passed the thanks along to Jesus under my breath as I made my way back into the kitchen.

We were getting tired.

"What do you think about 'concierge and straw boss' now?" Doris asked me.

"I think that Frank didn't have it quite right—except he probably had his own style, which he also said at the time, and maybe that worked for him. I also think we should talk about selling and moving on." I said. "Maybe move back to an island with golf courses and sandy beaches."

"I thought you were never going to suggest it," Doris replied, and I caught the joke. Word for word, it was what she'd said when I'd suggested buying a bed and breakfast in the first place.

"I think that we should give it at least three years though," Doris said, "which we nearly have, and I don't want to move away from Kentucky. Can't we find a nice little house around here?"

"Let's start to look," I said. "If we're planning a family Thanksgiving here again, maybe we could break the news to all and sundry at that time."

"Maybe," Doris responded. "At least let's see who wants to come for Thanksgiving."

I made the telephone calls.

"Are you kidding? We all have a ball when we come to Kentucky." This was Upper C.

"Of course, we'd love to come. Can we bring Emma's parents like we did last year?" This was the response from Lower C.

The only ones we had not yet heard from were Alec and, of course, Mary. We were surprised. Usually, they were the first to respond, and the lack of response seemed ominous. When the call came, it was from Mary. In a quiet, subdued voice, she said, "Your invitation brought everything to a head and made

Alec and I talk things over. I think you might already have an idea of what I'm going to say."

"Oh! Mary," Doris said.

Mary went on. "It seems that this is a little like a young man asking his potential parents-in-law for permission to marry their daughter. Except in this situation, this is the daughter-in-law asking her husband's parents' permission to divorce their son."

"You poor children," Doris said. "Has it come to this?"

"We still care about each other, but I can't keep up with Alec anymore. He used to make me laugh with all his antics, but I now find them childish and stupid. If we stay together any longer, we'll grow to dislike each other, and neither of us wants to go down that road."

"You know we've seen it coming, Mary, and feel sad for both of you," I said. "Are you sure that you are okay? Have you thought about counseling?"

"We're both okay, but it has to end and counseling is not an option. Alec is out of the house just now, but I told him that I was going to tell you. Obviously, I won't be coming for Thanksgiving, but I'm sure that Alec will. He'll call you soon, I'm sure."

"Do you want me to come to Columbus?" Doris asked. "Is there anything that we can do to help?"

"Doris, I'm going to love you and Derick forever, and in a strange way, I'm going to love your whacky son as well. I just can't live with him anymore, and now that the decision has been made, it is like a weight has been lifted and I'm feeling much, much better."

"You say that he will call?" Doris wanted to know.

"Oh yes. My guess is that he is a little embarrassed about everything and wanted me to break the news first."

"Mary, you must promise to stay in touch."

"I will."

As she put the phone down, Doris looked at me and said, "Is this what you expected?"

"It is," I replied, nodding my head. "Not what I wanted, but I think that both of us have known for a while that there was no future in that relationship, and she does sound adamant about 'no counseling.' They obviously don't want us or anybody to interfere."

"Thank goodness there are no children, and thank goodness that Mary is self-sufficient. She'll get over it and move on. Alec, on the other hand! What are we going to do about him?"

"What were we ever going to do about him?"

CHAPTER 12
Thanksgiving

Even without Mary, a family Thanksgiving was planned. Some folks were coming during the morning of Thanksgiving Day, others the day before, and Alec was coming the weekend before.

"You'll need help with the preparations," was his explanation. "And you know that Mary isn't joining us."

"We've talked to Mary," we told him. "Perhaps we'll get an opportunity to talk to you."

He showed up just after lunch on the Saturday prior to Thanksgiving and was well practiced in what he wanted to tell us.

"It didn't work between us," he said. "Mary was full of fun when we were first married, but then as time passed, she became more and more serious and wanted to take courses at work and make plans about getting on with our careers. I wanted us to start a family, but she was just interested in the serious stuff and not in favor with that even one little bit."

"You wanted a family?" Doris asked, amazed.

"Of course I did! Don't you remember all the good times that we had when the three us boys were growing up? But not Mary. She was an only child with alcoholic parents. Her dad passed out most nights, and her mother used to just leave him where he fell."

"I had heard that they drank," I replied, "but didn't think it was as bad as all that."

"Well, they're gone now," Alec said. Mary's parents had both died in an automobile accident before we met Mary. "Mary has nothing but bad memories of them, or so she says, and only wants a life of books and studying. She says that she thought that I would jolly her out of it, but that hasn't worked."

"Poor Mary," Doris said, sighing.

"Poor Mary! What about poor Alec? She'd doing exactly what she wants to do, and I've got to start over. At least I won't be married to a little blue nun any longer."

"What does that mean?" I asked.

"Figure it out, Pop. She didn't want children, she was completely off booze, she was out of bed before six every morning and in bed before ten every night. Do you see what I'm saying?"

"You mean *nothing?*"

He shook his head. "Nothing at all after the first few months we were married."

"No wonder he's been bouncing off the walls," I told Doris, after Alec had left.

"I blame us for not seeing it," Doris replied. "That poor boy and that poor girl, too, I suppose."

The next morning, Alec was up bright and early and in the kitchen before us and before Marla arrived. Marla brought Jack with her, and Alec made a great fuss of him. We didn't have a big crowd for breakfast, so I suggested that Doris and I leave it to Marla and Alec, and we'd go off and play with Jack.

"Great idea," Alec said. "But I'd like some time with Marla and Jack later if it is okay with you guys."

"Of course."

Doris went back to the bedroom to write letters and have some quiet time. Jack and I went off to climb on the old railroad stock in our nearby outdoor museum.

Jack was chatty. He told me about his favorite TV show and about how much he loved animals—*all* animals, even the fierce ones. He told me how much he loved his mother and how much he loved Uncle Alec.

"Do you see much of Uncle Alec?" I felt guilty quizzing a six-year-old boy.

"Sometimes," he said. "Sometimes when he comes to stay with us. Those are the really fun times."

Naturally, my curiosity was raised, but I couldn't put this little chap through the third degree—especially when later in the day I could go to the source: middle son Alec.

I wasted no time and cornered Alec at the first opportunity.

"Been seeing Marla then?" I casually asked him.

"Lately," he said. "Didn't see hardly anything of her until a couple of months ago."

"Been coming down to Kentucky at times other than when you stay at the inn?"

"Maybe once or twice," he said. "I usually spend time with her and Jack when I come to the inn though."

"What's going on?" I asked, tired of beating around the bush.

"Consenting adults," he replied. "Oh hell," he said, "this is all happening too quickly. We want to tell you but need to have it come together between the two of us first."

"This has nothing to do with what happened between you and Mary, has it? This isn't the reason why what happened between you Mary happened?" I was getting muddled in what I was saying.

"No Dad, calm down. Mary and I were dead as a couple six months after we married. We shouldn't have ever gotten married. Mary will admit that she thought that being married to me would change her and make her more outgoing and better able to enjoy life, but it just never happened. I really don't know why I married Mary. I think that I thought that it was the right thing to do and that it would make everybody happy. It didn't. It just made everybody sad." He shook his head. "I'll be honest. I like Marla. In fact, I like her a lot, but she's being cautious and who can blame her? I'm being cautious, and who can blame me? Then there's Jack to think about."

"We just don't want anyone to get upset. We don't need anybody getting hurt. And what do you mean when you say, 'Consenting adults?'"

"Oh God!! Father, what do you think that I mean? Dad, you and Mom are fine, but you still live in your generation. Things are different today. They are not necessarily better, but we're different people nowadays."

"I'm not sure that I like any of this."

"Neither of us is enjoying this conversation, that's for sure. Why don't we let it rest for a while?"

Thanksgiving plans were coming together. The daughters-in-law had been talking and making assignments, and Doris and I discussed who would sleep in which room. Doris wanted to be in charge of the turkey meal on Thanksgiving Day, while I wanted to arrange the entertainment. There were lists to be made, shopping to be done, and we needed to get the house ready.

It had become a tradition over the last three years for us to provide a Thanksgiving meal for Linda and Henry as well. The four of us would go off to the supermarket and buy ingredients plus a few extras to make sure that they had all that they needed. Alec said that he would like to be involved, that maybe he could buy them some wine. We said that he could help in any way that he wished, and after discussions with Linda and Henry, it was decided that a case of beer would be more to the recipients' taste than wine.

"I'm not too sure it's a good idea for them to have so much beer at one time," I told Alec. "They don't really understand the concept of budgeting, and if it's there, they might just drink it all in one session."

"You know, Pop, that's up to them."

"I know, Alec. I just worry about consequences and whether something can be avoided."

"Up to them, Pop," he said, shrugging his shoulders. "None of your business. Now I have a question. What would you say if I wanted to invite Marla and Jack to join us over Thanksgiving?"

"You mean for the meal?"

"No, I mean for *everything*—just as if they're family."

"Why are you asking me this without your mother being here?"

"Because I already asked her, and she said, 'Go and talk to your father.'"

"This isn't fair. I think the world of Marla, and Jack is my little buddy; however...." I was lost for words again. It was happening more frequently.

"If you're bothered because she isn't a family member, maybe one day that'll all change."

"What are you saying, Alec?"

"I'm saying that Marla and I are getting closer and closer, and Thanksgiving is a good time to introduce her to all the rest of the in-laws and out-laws."

"Are you happy, Alec?"

"Never been happier, Pop," he said, grinning.

"Do you mind if I talk to Marla?" I asked him, "without you being there? I need to feel sure that she's not being railroaded. I trust you, Alec, but your mother and I are a little vulnerable right now and any more 'situations' put on us might break the camel's back."

"No worries, mate," he said, with a twinkle in his eye.

I found Doris and told her that her dutiful son had done exactly as she'd asked and "asked his father" about inviting Marla.

"And what did you say?"

"I said that I wanted to talk to Marla, have a heart-to-heart without Alec nearby."

"You know that everything that you say to her will get back to Alec."

"Probably, but that's a good thing. You and I don't have secrets. Do you want to be a part of the conversation?"

"No, I'll be the back up plan in case it's needed."

"What does that mean, Doris?"

"Absolutely nothing," she said. "I think both of us want something good to happen. You handle it first, and if you need help, ask. That way, we get two shots of going for it, and I'm much better at patching and cleaning than you are. Just remember, if you get any sense that Marla is being coerced, put an end to it."

I called Marla. "Lunch?" I asked.

"Just with you, Derick?" she wanted to know.

"Just me," I replied.

"I'm not in trouble, am I?" she asked.

"Not you, love," I answered, and we made our arrangements.

We planned to meet in Lexington, as I wanted to pick up some party supplies for Thanksgiving. We both agreed that we liked Italian food, so picked a small restaurant just off Nicholasville road. This particular restaurant did major business during the dinner hour, probably because they provided live entertainment but weren't terribly busy for lunch, which I thought would be a better environment for our talk.

As I drove into Lexington, the reverse of the drive that Doris and I had made over three years ago, I found myself thinking back over our bed and breakfast experience and wondering whether it had all been worthwhile. There had been good times for sure, and our lives were not boring. We had plenty to do. But although the economy was turning around, we had made very little if any money during those three years. The bank had helped us when we needed it, but we'd borrowed more than we should have to buy the inn in the first place and were now stuck with a hefty monthly payment. To the bank's credit, they'd reduced the interest rate so the monthly payment was less. But they say the reduction is only temporary. They, too, can read the numbers—probably better than we can. Most certainly they don't want to own a bed and breakfast while we're in it making, albeit reduced, payments. Maybe if that appraisal hadn't been so glowing, we wouldn't have been doing this now.

I also thought about the effect that the bed and breakfast life was having on Doris and me. We'd been lucky—married for nearly fifty years. Most of our early married life had been spent on forwarding our respective careers and raising the family. There were many distractions, and between the boys and our jobs, we'd had no time to get bored with each other's company. Now, not only were we together 24/7 but we were working together, too. Some of the natural aging processes was creeping into our relationship, Doris was getting harder of hearing, and I was getting more short-tempered, especially at being asked to repeat something that I thought I had just said quite clearly in the first place. Plus, even with help, running an inn is hard work.

Still, the other side of that coin is that, as noted before, we're not bored, we have purpose, we meet the most interesting people, and we are alive. If only we could figure out a way to get a break every now and then while knowing that the inn was still being run to our standards.

Why I had all of these thoughts in my head on my way to meet Marla, I'll never know. I should have been thinking about what I was going to say to her. I was already regretting having gotten myself into this situation.

I arrived at the restaurant a little early, parked, and went in to get a quiet table. The light inside was not as bright as the late morning sun, and it took a couple of seconds to adjust. When I could see clearly again, I noticed that Marla had beaten me to the restaurant and was sitting at a corner table smiling in my direction. As I walked toward her, I looked around the rest of the dining room to be sure that we had the best seat for our meeting. Marla's smile had turned to a grin.

"He's not here, if that's what you're looking around for," she said.

"What....? Oh, Alec." I shook my head. "No, I didn't expect him, but then again with Alec one never quite knows what to expect." I sat down. "How are you?"

"I'm fine, Derick."

The waitress was right behind me as I took a seat on the opposite side of the table from Marla. The waitress gave the usual "welcome to our restaurant" speech and asked if we wanted anything to drink before we ordered lunch. It was common for me to just ask for soda water. Doris enjoyed a midday glass of wine better than I.

"I'll have the same," Marla added, but then I changed my mind.

"No, I'll have a glass of Chianti, if you have it by the glass?"

"We do."

"Marla, will you change your mind also?" I asked.

"Oh sure, why not," she said. "I've only the remotest idea of what this lunch is all about. Possibly it's my last lunch with an Anderson, so better to go out in a blaze of glory."

I continued talking. "Marla, this was my cockamamie idea of getting some time to talk to you away from the rest of those involved. You are not being fired, or quizzed, or anything. If you prefer, I'll be the only person to talk. You can just sit there, mute. We want you to work for us forever, but there are other issues that have come up, and I just wanted to be sure that you are comfortable with . . . well, everything."

The waitress returned with the wine and asked if we were ready to order.

"My friend here has lost her voice," I said. "I'll order for both of us."

Even behind her heavily beveled glasses, I could see that Marla's eyes had opened as wide as they could go. I also detected a wry smile on her lips.

"The lunch special is Shrimp Diablo?" I asked the waitress, as I studied the menu.

"Yes."

"I think that will be fine for us both. Marla, just nod if you want the special." Marla, eyes still huge, nodded.

"Good then," I said to the waitress. "Two specials please," and with that the waitress was gone.

Marla stared at me and said, "Derick Anderson, you are certifiably crazy. I can see now where Alec gets it."

"Alec," I replied. "Hum, oh yes, Alec is on the list for today's discussion. He's far crazier than me though."

"I'm not sure," Marla answered.

"Marla, are you happy working with us? Is there anything that we do wrong or anything that we can improve upon to make life easier for you?"

"I'm happy," Marla said. "Are you happy with me?"

"Very," I said, nodding. "I—actually *we*, since this includes Doris—think that you are as close to perfect as one can get, and we don't want to lose you, but something has come up, and we wanted to be sure that you are happy with it."

"Are you talking about Alec?" Marla asked.

"Yes, I am. In fact, I spend a lot of time talking about Alec." I went on. "Has he been taking advantage of you in any way?"

"Alec, taking advantage of *me?*" she replied. "Oh no!" She shook her head. "I worry that *I'm* taking advantage of *him*."

"Go on."

"You've never asked, and I appreciate that, but you must be a little curious about me, where I come from and where Jack came from. This is good wine by the way," she said, lifting her glass. "Perhaps that's why I'm opening up to you. My mom and dad are older, both officially retired, and not well off financially. Mom found a part-time job working at the library. I'm an only child and, looking back, it must have been a great disappointment to them when I told them in my last year of high school that I was not going on to college; instead, I was going to get married. I used to get good grades, and it was always expected that I would go on and be the first in our family to get a degree. They were disappointed, but they were also naïve and had no idea that I had been swept off my feet by Robbie. Good time, Robbie; let's have a ball, Robbie. Maybe it was me who was naïve."

We were so engrossed in conversation that we hadn't noticed the waitress standing next to the table with our entrees. The waitress had a puzzled look on her face as she stood there listening to the woman described as being unable to talk chattering away. We nodded at her with a smile when her presence was realized and leaned back so that she could put the plates in front of us.

"Is there anything else I can get for you?" she asked, looking pointedly at Marla.

Marla just shook her head, so the waitress said, "Bon appitito," and left.

"I'm sorry, Marla," I said. "I shouldn't have come up with the deaf and dumb thing. I'll apologize to the sweet young thing later. Go on with your story."

"Not much of a story," Marla said. "Robbie and I did get married, and in no time came the Iraq war. Robbie volunteered for the Army. He was somewhat changed after we were married, not quite so much fun. It's difficult to describe, as he was off to war. I didn't think any of the changes that I saw in him were real. Am I talking too much?"

"No, not at all," I said. "And you know, you don't have to tell me all this if you'd prefer not to."

She shook her head. "I want you to know—especially about Jack. You've been so good to him in the time that we have known each other."

"Was Robbie killed in the war?"

"Oh no! Robbie is still around, I think, but then again maybe he was killed in the war. The Robbie who came back from Iraq wasn't the same Robbie as the young man that I married. He did two tours of duty, and Jack was born during the second tour. Robbie was funny about it. He said that he didn't want to be a father and that I shouldn't have gotten pregnant. He even questioned whether he was the father. What's more, he did all that over the phone and the Internet while he was overseas. I'm not sure that he would have come home for Jack's birth even if it had been permitted. He made no effort to do so."

"You were by yourself when Jack was born?"

"No, Mom and Dad were with me, and heaven only knows where Robbie was. The war changed Robbie. Who knows, perhaps I'd changed, too, but our lives as a couple was disintegrating rapidly. Robbie took no interest whatsoever in Jack. He started to drink, and he was not a nice drunk. I think that he did drugs as well. One thing led to another, and he became more and more detached." She paused to take a sip of wine.

"The first time he hit me was over nothing, and as I remember, he wasn't even drunk at the time. The only work he could find was on a construction site in Frankfort. He worked there as a laborer. He wasn't happy. The other men were constantly after him to come out with them after work and chase girls. He was always broke, but even if he had only five dollars in his pocket, he would buy lottery tickets. He never won. I became the target. I was the reason everything had gone wrong for him, and Jack was only fuel for the fire."

"What did you do?" I asked.

"Moved out, moved in with Mom and Dad. I even took out a restraining order because I was worried about Jack, but it turned out to be unnecessary. Robbie moved away. He told everybody that he was taking off for Alaska, where he said he could make good money. But the last that I heard was that he only got as far as Nevada. He and I are divorced now, so I don't keep up with him. I've heard that he got married again, and then divorced again. Somebody told me that he got into drugs big time, and they thought he was doing time somewhere in one of those God forsaken desert prisons. It's all over, and I'm not very proud of myself, but you bought the wine and the wine loosened my tongue and this is the consequence."

"Marla, I'm sorry," I said.

"Oh, don't be," she said, waving a hand at me. "There's nothing to be sorry about. I've got a fantastic young son out of the relationship; I got to be close to my parents, who were like rocks through it all; and I now know enough not to make the same mistake again."

"Are you hinting that Alec might be a 'same mistake again'?"

"No. No, not at all. What do you know about Alec and me?" Marla asked.

"He seems to be very fond of you and wants us to ask you to our family Thanksgiving."

"He does? He hasn't mentioned that."

"You know all about Alec and Mary and that they are now separated?" I enquired.

We were aware that our waitress had returned to clear away the used plates, which we let her do.

"Our waitress seems like a nice young woman," I said to Marla, "but she does have a habit of creeping up quietly so that you don't know she's there."

"Maybe it's you getting engrossed in conversation."

"Maybe, but let's get back to Thanksgiving. Actually, let's get back to Alec first. He can be a handful, you know."

"So can you, Derick," Marla replied. "I think that Doris is a saint."

"You know what I mean. We don't want to see either of you hurt. And there is Jack to think of," I said.

"Derick, Alec and I have become close, and he has shared a lot with me and Jack over the past months," Marla said. "I have seen Alec struggle with the situation between him and Mary and have tried not to interfere in any way. But it just wasn't right between the two of them. It seems to me that Mary didn't want the kinds of things that Alec wanted, and that Alec has given up on trying to be somebody that he's not. I'm not sure what he has shared with you, but I get the impression that he only married because it was the thing to do, not because he wanted to. That he tried everything to make Mary happy, nothing has succeeded, and now he believes, as crazy as it seems, that the only way for Mary to achieve any kind of happiness is for him to leave and make out that he is the bad guy."

I looked around the restaurant. "Are you sure that he is not here listening to all of this?"

"He's not here, Derick, and he doesn't know how I feel."

"But he can still be a handful," I said.

"Just like his dad. This acorn didn't fall too far from the tree, and as I said, Doris is a saint. Besides, Jack thinks that the sun rises and sets because of Alec."

"What about Thanksgiving?" I was going to say more but stopped because the silent waitress had returned with the bill. I smiled and handed her my credit card. "I wonder what she's telling them in the kitchen?" I added.

"Derick, I'd love to come for Thanksgiving, but that wouldn't be fair to my mom and dad. Thanksgiving being such a family time."

Now I felt a fool. Doris would have established all of the background first and not put her foot in her mouth, as I had just done.

"I'm sorry, Marla," I said. "I should have thought—we could ask them, too."

"They're impossibly shy," Marla said. "I doubt that they would accept, especially as you will have a house full of people who they don't know."

"I am embarrassed," I went on. "I should have thought about your parents. I don't know anything about them."

"Dad is retired. He used to work at the printing company in town but got laid off. He couldn't find anything else, so he elected to take his pension. Mom has this part-time job at the library. They don't have a lot of money, but they get by."

"Doris goes to the library at least once a week; maybe she knows your mom," I said.

"Maybe, but it's never come up in any conversation that I've had with either of them."

The silent waitress was once again standing over my shoulder with the credit card receipt to sign.

"I'm going to give her a good tip," I said to Marla. "Perhaps she'll buy some new shoes that make a noise, or squeak or something."

"Derick," Marla replied, "give her a good tip because she's a good waitress. Where are we going now, and what is it that you want me to help you with?"

"The party shop," I announced. "I want to get some decorations to dress up the house for a day-after-Thanksgiving Day party. I thought that I would ask everybody to dress as either a princess or a pirate, and we'll play games. You know, that sort of thing."

"Acorns and trees again," Marla observed. "I'll be happy to help you."

When I got home and was showing Doris all of the decorations and prizes that I'd bought, I told her about my conversation with Marla and how I'd put my foot into it regarding her parents.

"What's her mother's name?" Doris asked.

"I didn't ask," I replied.

"Men!" was her only response.

We had one big group of guests for three days the weekend prior to Thanksgiving. They were all older and had taken to spending mini-vacations together in different parts of the southeast. They brought bicycles and would cycle around country lanes during the day, then eat in some fancy restaurant in the evening. They were very nice, but maybe because they were the only guests, they tended to take over the house as if it were their own. They missed the concept that some parts of the house were private and that there were some times of the day when the innkeepers wanted to be alone. Some of them didn't hear too well either, and we had to raise our voices when talking to them, so they raised theirs in response. It was tiring and made worse by not having a hideaway, since the guests were everywhere. Rudely, we christened them, "The Zombies" behind their backs.

On top of all this, Alec showed up wanting to know what projects I had for him. A pretty poor excuse, I thought, as it seemed obvious that he had come to see Marla and not us. Alec had bought a motorcycle, which he drove down to Kentucky for this visit. He had spent so much time at the inn over the past months that most of his wardrobe and other essentials were already in storage with us. Turning up on a motorcycle seemed fitting, as he could travel light. He was very proud of his motorcycle and tried to tell me about all of the features—overhead this and supercharged that. I wasn't even remotely interested, so I quieted him down by saying, "I asked Marla about Thanksgiving, but she can't make it."

"Yeah, I heard. It's a shame."

"She's a very nice young woman, that Marla," I continued. "But sometimes I think that she hides behind those thick eyeglasses of hers."

"I'm sure that she does," Alec said. "I don't blame her. Anyway, she's quite different when she takes them off."

Doris announced that she had had enough talk about motorcycles and eyeglasses. She needed to get out of the house, away from the wandering "zombie guests" and away from her husband and whacky son—just for an hour or so.

"Do you have any idea of what I mean?" she said.

"We'll hold down the fort while you're gone," I told her. She didn't grace us with a reply; she just took off.

"Alec, if you'd like to supervise Linda and Henry for a while, I want to shop for a nice meal for the three of us tonight," I said. "Keep your eye on Henry. He acts like he knows what he's doing, but he often gets it wrong and matters finish up worse than before he started.

"It's a shame that Marla and Jack can't come for Thanksgiving. Have you met her parents?" I asked.

"Sure have," he said. "I've met them a couple of times. They're nice folks. Keep to themselves and are real quiet."

"Alec, next to you, a marching band is quiet. Whatever. Keep your eye on Linda and Henry. I think they might be feuding, and I don't want that spilling over into the inn."

I decided on steaks for dinner—smallish filets that I liked to prepare by browning them on the stovetop and then cooking them in a hot oven. After taking them out to rest, I prepared a sauce out of the brown bits left in the pan. It had become a family favorite. The grandchildren called them Grandpa's Steaks, which pleased me. Sometimes I'd bake some potatoes to go with them, but I decided on a packet of scalloped cheese potatoes instead, as the steaks were on the smallish side. I was getting to be reasonably efficient in the kitchen.

We were late eating because the "zombies" were wandering all over the house trying to organize themselves about where to go out for their evening meal. They really were nice people, not zombies at all, but Doris's nicknames often stick. Finally, they all landed in one spot, and their leader pushed them into cars and headed them out to a local restaurant. I commandeered the kitchen for my creation while Alec prepared the table and Doris fixed drinks. It all came together, and the three of us sat down to eat.

"Betty Rollins," Doris said, right out of the blue.

Alec and I looked at each other nervously, neither knowing what to answer and wondering whether Doris was having a senior moment.

"I give up," I said eventually. "Was that a question in Trivial Pursuit?"

"No," Doris replied. "Betty Rollins is Marla's mother. I've been talking to her at the library."

Alec and I both had "I wonder what's coming next" looks on our faces.

"I've known Betty for quite a while now," Doris said. "She is very good at her job in the library. She knows the sorts of books I like to read and makes recommendations from time to time. It's funny, but we've never discussed family before today. I had no idea that she was Marla's mother, although she seemed to know all about us, and she actually likes you, Alec."

Alec and I were still at a loss for words.

Doris was not at such a loss.

"They're coming," she said. "Not on Thanksgiving Day, but she said that they will come to the party on the day after. I told them that they didn't have to dress up in a ridiculous costume. You're okay with that, aren't you, Derick?"

"Yes, he is," Alec said, before I could open my mouth.

"Betty was a little reluctant when I first mentioned it," Doris went on, "but it turns out that they go to Mandy's restaurant at times, so I told her that I would invite Mandy if that would make it easier. She jumped at that idea, so I said that I would let her know whether Mandy was coming or not. Then I went to Mandy's. I told her the situation and invited Mandy to the party as well. She's busy because the restaurant is open but said that she would come for a short while to make it easier on everybody. It further turns out that Mandy's mother—you remember Elsie, don't you, Derick?—well Elsie is in town for Thanksgiving, so she will be invited as well."

Bad and embarrassing memories flooded through my mind. Eventually I stuttered, "Elsie is coming to the party?"

"Yes, she is," Doris said. "You're okay with that, too, aren't you, Derick?"

"What's going on here?" Alec wanted to know.

"Only that your father flashed Elsie when she had kindly offered to help us get started in our first few weeks here," Doris said.

"Pop did *what?*" Alec said, his mouth dropping open.

"I didn't flash the woman," I said, defending myself.

"Well, what do you call parading around naked in front of her, then?" Doris asked.

"Pop did *what?*" Alec asked again.

"I was in our private suite, moving from the bathroom to the dressing room to get dressed, when I came across Elsie—or rather Elsie came across me," I tried to explain.

"Oh, this is priceless," Alec said. "Do tell more."

"There's nothing more to tell. I didn't know that she was there, so we came across each other, so to speak."

"You weren't even wearing a towel?" Alec asked.

"I didn't know she was there!"

"Bare ass naked?" Alec said, pressing forward.

"Bare ass naked," I acknowledged.

"Oh, so priceless," Alec said. "Do the others know?"

"Of course not, Alec. Why would I tell anybody a story like that?"

"Well, they will probably know pretty soon. Oh, this is going to be a good Thanksgiving! And she's coming to the party. Priceless." Then Alec asked, "What did she say?"

"Something about now being a part of the family," I answered. "You're not going to make too much of this, are you, and embarrass the children?"

"I won't embarrass the children, I promise, but the children's parents, my brothers and sisters-in-law, are going to have a wonderful time with the story."

"Oh God!" I said, throwing up my hands. "All I need now is for Miles and Grayson to show up to make the whole bloody thing complete."

Doris had had enough. "We now need to ask Marla and Jack."

Doris looked at Alec. "If you ask them, perhaps they'll say yes."

"Oh, they'll say yes, I'm sure," Alec said, smiling. "Well done, Momma san. Haven't lost your touch, have you?"

"Just doing my job!" Doris said. "Perhaps when you talk to Marla and tell her that her mother and I have figured out who is who. Then ask her if she and Jack will come to party with her Mom and Dad."

"I'll do it right now. Be back in a flash, if you get my meaning, Pop." And with that, Alec was gone.

It was a "zombie" morning, and even the "zombie" leader was getting frustrated at trying to keep them together. They just wandered everywhere. Mostly it was a lot like counting goldfish; they never stood still. One by one, they showed up for breakfast, and we thought that we had a full compliment seated around the table, but one was missing.

The leader, who was beginning to get more and more frazzled said, "Who's missing? Somebody has to know whether their partner is not with them."

They started to look around the table at each other and shake their heads from side to side. Nobody claimed to know who the missing party was. The leader was getting beside herself.

Doris and I stood by, bemused by the whole affair. We offered to go and look for the missing party, but the offer was rejected with a firm, "No."

"Surely somebody knows who is missing." The leader was pleading with them now, but still no response.

Slowly, one-by-one, they got up from the table and began their zombie shuffle around the house, presumably looking for their lost soul. The leader just collapsed and held her head in her hands. I thought that she was about to cry.

"You don't think?" Doris asked me.

"Alec," I replied.

"Yes, Alec."

"With this lot and with Alec, anything is possible," I said. "Pretty bad combination. I'll go and try to find him."

Sure enough, I found Alec with one of the zombies in the garage showing off his new motorcycle. I couldn't tell whether this was one of the group who had made it to the table or if this was the missing party. There was a sameness about the way they all looked. I presumed he was the missing party; however, and invited him for his meal.

"How about breakfast?" I asked

"We can get our breakfast here?" was the reply, more of a question really.

"Yes you can. Follow me. Alec, can you help round up everybody else and then help your mother, please."

At last the head count around the table was correct. We dished up Eggs Benedict, which was very well received. The leader kept close tabs on everybody, corralled them into their van, paid the bill, and bade us, "Thank You and Farewell." The van made its way down the drive, and we breathed a sigh of relief that the house could be our home for a few days, family only.

I fished out the "No Vacancy" sign to hang outside, which would hopefully stop people from just casually dropping in.

It was Wednesday, and one-by-one each member of the family and extended family arrived. It was wonderful to hear the voices of children around the house again. There were screams of delight as brothers and daughters-in-law greeted each other; raucous laughter as they told stories about each other; and lots of hugs and kisses. The boys mostly drank beer and their wives drank wine. Everyone had agreed prior to driving down that they wanted Doris and me to have a break, so assignments had been made for preparation of the meal the next day, and that night, everybody wanted pizza delivery from the local deli in Versailles.

"I have a couple of announcements," I told the group when we were all gathered. "Mary is not joining us this year, and we will have some additions for the party on Friday."

"Get on with it," Alec said. "They all know about Mary and me. Let's not dwell on that, please."

I nodded. "Okay, I won't. Some of you know Marla, who helps us out from time to time. Actually, *most* of the time. Well, Marla and her son Jack and Marla's parents are coming to the party on Friday. Mandy from the restaurant down the road and her mother are also dropping in for a while."

The more the merrier was the general feeling of the group. Those who had met Marla in the past had taken to her and were glad that she would be at the party.

"Wait until you hear the story about Mandy's mom," Alec said, interrupting.

I cut him off. "One more thing to tell you. Your mother and I are feeling a little tired of our bed and breakfast gig. It's getting to be both tiring and demanding, so we think that we might make a change."

This time, the response was silence.

Then, "Are you okay?" "You're not ill are you?" "What's happened? We thought that you enjoyed it?" The questions came at us fast and furious.

I held up my hands. "We are okay, and we are not ill, and we do enjoy running a bed and breakfast. But every now and then, we need to get away from it. It's a 24/7 occupation running an inn, even with all of the help that we have."

"Can't we help?" "Isn't there something that we can do?"

"You all have your own lives, and your mother and I will never impose on you in that way. Thanks for the offers, but selling the inn is probably the best solution."

"When?"

"It's not yet decided," I replied. "Now let's boogey and have the best Thanksgiving ever." I raised my glass. "Cheers everybody."

Through the crowd, I noticed that Doris had a faraway, sad look in her eye. I thought that perhaps she was having second thoughts about selling the inn. I know that's how I felt.

Noise, music, laughter, good food, good booze—it was fabulous, and the old house really came into its own, as if it, too, was a part of our family. Were we doing the right thing by moving on? Everything fit here. Everything fell into place. There were great smells from the kitchen, warmth from the fire, smiling faces—it was wonderful. Occasional cries from the youngest ones when they tripped or otherwise bumped themselves, but it all just added to the ambiance of a close family enjoying each other's company. Too much turkey, stuffing to die for, overwhelming vegetables, fabulous gravy, and one too many spoonfuls of desert. It was turning into the best Thanksgiving ever—just as we had hoped.

We waddled from the table to the nearest TV. Another good thing about owning a B&B was that there were television sets all over the place—enough for a choice of football games, children's TV, or video games. The weather had been kind, so we were also able to get a small: pick-up baseball game underway in the paddock for those who wished to play. Stories were told about Thanksgivings and Christmases in the past, everybody got to be the butt of one story or another, and nobody was left out. Alec took center stage and brought the house down with a greatly exaggerated retelling of my encounter with Elsie. It was just a fabulous day.

Friday morning, and we were greeted by a drizzly day that was a little on the chilly side. I had planned a nine hole golf tournament for those who wanted to play, but I was going off the idea because of the weather. Most of the others were in agreement, except Alec, who still wanted to play. He was eventually persuaded to relax, and even though the weather cleared as the morning progressed, we just had a lazy time in the house with the newspaper and coffee. I noticed that cars were gathering for a funeral at the funeral home next door and was a little put out. I thought that we could start our party off with a parade down our driveway; however, I didn't want to upset the bereaved next door with the sight of pirates and princesses marching to military band music from a boom box.

A sandwich lunch from leftovers and cold cuts was served up by Doris and her our daughters-in-law. Alec had prepared a bubble and squeak from leftover vegetables, which I must say was pretty good. It was then nap time for an hour or so prior to getting into our costumes for the party.

I was the first dressed in a brightly colored woman's silk blouse, which I had purchased at the thrift store for about three dollars. I had some tatty old trousers, a patch over one of my eyes, and was bare footed. It wasn't much of a costume, but I was showing spirit for the children, and at least I thought that I looked like a pirate. Doris looked fabulous as a princess, and we had started to decorate the living room as the others began to show up. It was amazing. All of the children had dressed as one would expect given their gender, just as their grandparents had. The boys dressed as pirates and the girls dressed as princesses. The adults, on the other hand, seemed to have more fun by cross-dressing. Most of the women, not all, dressed as pirates, and most of the men became princesses. The house rocked with laughter as each new person showed up and showed off their costumes. The little girls were all so pretty, the little boys all dashing, and the adults all ridiculous—including me, even though I was gender specific.

As it was inappropriate for us to march outside, I decided to direct our parade through the downstairs part of the house. I organized and lined everybody up in the living room, and from there, we were to march into and through the dining room, on into the kitchen, where we turned right through a narrow space into the garden room. Another right turn into the long hall marched us toward the front door, then a final right turn to be back in the living room. When all was ready, I had The Ohio State Marching Band recording of "Hang On Sloopy" turned up loud on a boom box, which I carried on my shoulder. I positioned myself as the last person in the parade so that the music drifted over everybody else. Off we went, music blaring out, swinging our arms, singing away. *"Hang on, Sloopy, sloopy hang on. O.H.I.O. Hang on, Sloopy, sloopy hang on."* We were singing at the tops of our voices and waving to imaginary onlookers.

I didn't hear the front doorbell. None of us did. We were making way too much noise. We joyously marched through the dining room, through the kitchen, passed through the garden room, and were making our triumphant march down the long hall toward the front door, singing as loud as we could, when the door opened and standing there with "deer in the headlights" eyes were all of them: Marla, Jack, Marla's mother and father, Mandy, and Elsie. They stared at us. It must have been quite a shock to them—pirates and princesses waving their hands, singing their heads off, marching directly toward them. To their credit, they didn't turn and run.

Doris was first to the rescue. "Switch off the music, Derick," she shouted; however, I was at the back of the parade, and I didn't hear her at first.

Alec heard and took up the cry. "Pop, Pop, the music. Turn off the music."

Then others joined in until I got the message and switched off the machine.

"What an unfortunate welcome," Doris said to our guests, who were standing still, stunned, on the front doorstep. "But do come on in." Doris motioned for them to come inside. "Let me make the introductions."

We all retreated to the living room while the new arrivals gingerly came into the hall, peering around with quizzical looks on their faces. I was worried that they might not stay.

Alec to the rescue. "Welcome to our crazy family," he said. "We don't usually do this on Fridays. Usually on Friday we get wild and do really stupid things, all of course, at the general encouragement and instigation of the patriarch and leader of our pack, Mr. Derick Anderson." He grinned and pointed my way.

Jaw open, I was at a loss for words, but I tried at least to smile in welcome to these new folks.

Alec went on and said to the family, "Folks, please meet Marla, her son Jack, and Marla's mother and father, Betty and Herbert Rollins. Then, of course, Mandy and, I'm guessing, Mandy's beautiful mother Elsie."

Things were starting to calm down, and that remark about Elsie helped to further break the ice. Most started to smile and a few shouts of "Hi" and "Welcome" came from around the room.

Alec was especially kind to Jack. "Hey, young man, I've got something for you." And with that, he produced a pirate's hat that he had hidden behind a chair.

"I didn't want you to feel left out if the others were all dressed up," he said. "You don't have to wear it if you don't want to."

Jack took the hat and put it on, much to the relief of Marla, then some of the other children came over and started talking to him, and in no time he was joining in with them.

Betty and Herbert were quiet, but Doris had moved over next to them and was trying to make them feel at home. She asked if she could get them something to nibble on or to drink. Marla stood next to her parents and smiled as they started to relax and gradually join in.

Mandy and Elsie were not shy at all and soon were talking to everybody, accepting wine and finger food. It was difficult for anybody not to feel welcome with this group, especially dressed in fancy costumes as we all were.

I thought that I should make sure that we included everybody and wanted to reinforce Alec's original introductions, so I banged a spoon on the side of my glass and waited for quiet.

"The children don't have to stay, but I want to formally welcome our new guests," I said, and with that the kids all took off for various and different parts of the house. Jack included.

"Marla has been helping us here for quite a while now," I said. "She feels like family, so it is only appropriate that she be included in our party. Her mother and father graciously accepted our invitation also, and we are so pleased to have their company. Some of you might already know Mandy from her restaurant down the street, but you might not know her mother."

With that, Elsie interrupted me. "Derick, I know some of you, and you must remember that I worked here for a short time. We were just like family back then."

I started to blush.

Elsie didn't stop there. "Derick went to a lot of trouble at that time to show that I was a member of the family."

And Alec of course got the connection.

"Member," he called out. "Member, I get it, Elsie. Well, we now all know the story of how old Pop here went to great lengths to make you feel at home."

"The lengths weren't that great," Elsie responded, and then the two of them collapsed with laughter. Others, too, were beginning to catch on, and in the end, laughter overtook all of us, including me. Nothing was sacred anymore.

Even though Mandy and Elsie had to leave for the dinner hour at Mandy's restaurant, which promised to be a busy evening for them, our party continued well into the evening. We had plenty of wine, too much food, and more fun than ever playing silly guessing games, charades, hide-and-go-seek, and musical chairs. No tears from the children, which was a bonus since one can usually count on one bump or maybe two to invoke a cry. Alec was acting more responsibly than usual, still the heart and soul of the party but nothing over the top or too outrageous. He was very attentive toward Marla and Jack, making sure that they were appropriately included but not pushing them. Not that he needed to be protective; they seemed to fit right in with the rest of the group as though they were born to be there. Betty and Herbert stayed quiet, but one could tell that this was their nature. They stayed almost to the end of the party and had spent most of their time smiling at the antics of others. Doris and I couldn't call it a day until Betty and Herbert left, and honestly, we were more than a little relived when they announced that it was time for them to go.

"I'll drive you home," Marla said to her parents.

"Let me do it," Alec asked. "Better yet, why don't they take your car, Marla, and I'll see that you and Jack get home safely when you're ready to go."

"Yes," Marla said, nodding, "that's a good idea. You take my car, Mom and Dad."

I don't think that Marla's parents were given much choice in this decision, but they agreed, said goodbye to everybody, thanked Doris and me, and left. Doris and I, along with some of the in-laws, decided to call it a night not long after, leaving the party and the youngsters to get on with the rest of the evening by themselves. To shouts of "Thank you" and "Sleep tight," we made our way to our bedroom.

Once in bed, Doris asked, "What do you think, Derick?"

Oh no, I thought. *No deep conversations at this time of night.* I was exhausted. "About what?" I said.

"About Alec," Doris answered. "Have you ever seen him so happy?"

"He used to be the happiest soul I knew when he was kid," I responded.

"Well, I think that he's got his mojo back. I hope that Mary has found what she is looking for as well." And with that, Doris put an end to the conversation.

Saturday morning, and we learned that Jack had just tumbled in with the rest of the children and fallen asleep with them somewhere in the inn. Alec had taken Marla home and not returned. It was leaving day for the rest of the family, and some of them were up and in various stages of packing bags and cars getting ready to return home. It is always sad when we say goodbye to them, and especially sad this time because our Thanksgiving break had been such a great success. We still had the inn closed off through Sunday, and this was still only Saturday, so we did have a couple of days before we had to put our innkeeper's hats on again, and we were only partially busy over the next few weeks.

Alec and Marla showed up before any of the others had to leave, so the house was full again with much activity before goodbyes were said.

"Are you leaving today?" I asked Alec.

"I want to talk to you and Mom," he said, "but no, I'm not leaving today. Let's have our chat after the others have left."

One by one, each car was loaded, and one by one, each pulled out of the drive and headed back mostly to Ohio. As the last one left, Alec said, "I could go for a bloody Mary. We've still got some left, haven't we?"

"I'm sure that we do," I answered. "Fix four if Marla is staying."

"No, she's not," Alec replied. "I'll fix three."

Doris looked at me and said, "Now what? Why is Marla leaving? What's happened between the two of them?"

"Doris," I said, "why are you looking on the dark side? Why do you think that something has happened between them?"

"Because I was hoping that they were going to tell us good news, that's all."

With that, Alec walked back into the room with Bloody Marys.

"Great Thanksgiving, Mom and Dad," he said. "Everybody had a great time."

"Thanks Alec, but a lot of the credit goes to you. You were a marvelous help," I replied.

"We all had quite a chat last night, the family, after you and the other parents went to bed," he told us. "We made some decisions, and we all want you two to know what's on our minds."

"Go on."

"First, I'm leaving Ohio. I have no life up there any longer, and I can get a nurse's job down here quite easily."

"Oh, you're moving down here, are you?" I interjected.

"Pop, come on, you're not blind. I adore Marla and Jack and want nothing more than to be with them all day and every day. Marla says that she feels the same. She's telling her parents right now at the same time that I'm telling you so as to not play favorites, of which there aren't any anyway."

"Oh, thank God," Doris said. "I'm so happy for all three of you."

"But that's not the only reason I wanted to have this chat," Alec said. "That was going to happen anyway. What I wanted to say . . . what the rest of the family wants me to say, is that we don't want you to sell the inn. We know that it's hard for you, and we know that you need a break every now and then, but we also know that you love it most of the time, and if you do sell, you will be bored and probably make all our lives a living hell. So, with everybody's agreement, we want you to stay on, but we want you to let Marla and I take over from time to time, even most of the time, to sort of ease the burden. What do you think?"

"Whew, you've said a lot there," I said to Alec.

"What do you think?" he replied.

"The offer is tempting, but your mother and I need to talk it over."

"I understand. Now I need to go and ask Betty and Herbert for their daughter's hand in marriage."

"Busy morning you've got going," I observed. "Quit a job, move to new state, find a job, propose marriage, and help your parents out in their dotage."

"Good thing that I've got a motorbike then, with all this going on it makes getting around so much easier without using too much gas."

"I don't understand what that means?" I asked.

"It means nothing, Pop. You and Mom talk. I'll be back later." And with that, he was gone.

Doris and I just looked at each other, lost for words at first. Eventually, I managed to mumble, "What do you think?"

"Too much going on for me," she replied. "What do *you* think?"

"Same as you," I answered, "but my initial inclination is to say yes to all of the above. This might be our chance to move into 'Semi-retirement'—the best of all worlds. Something to do without the worries of having it all to do. Keep an interest in life, get a pay check, but no downside if the money doesn't come in."

"Semi-retirement," answered Doris. "I do like the sound of that, and even though somewhere in the back of my mind I seem to remember hearing almost the exact words being used to sell me on the idea of buying the inn in the first place, I still like the sound of it."

"Semi-retirement it is then?" I asked

"Semi-retirement," she replied.

Addendum

When guests check in to our bed and breakfast, I ask them if they would like a short tour and to learn a little about the history of the house and the people who have lived here. The real inn—"1823 Historic Rose Hill Inn," renamed Primrose Hill Inn in this novel and pictured on the front—is a fascinating old building. Built in 1823 as a plantation federal-style house and extensively remodeled in the 1870s, the inn has served as a family home prior to the Civil War, with slave quarters and a separate kitchen. It was also a hospital during the War Between the States (we even have bloodstains on the floor where wounded soldiers waited for attention); a gracious Victorian mansion, with stained glass windows and a Waterford crystal chandelier; a doctor's office after World War II; before becoming a family home again prior to being remolded into a bed and breakfast in the 1980s. My real life wife (Gill) and I have owned and operated the inn since 2007.

During the course of the tour and telling of the history, I'm often asked how Gill and I came to be in the inn. It seems that there are as many people interested in what makes innkeepers tick as people interested in the background of the house. I thought that I would write a brief history of us as well as that of the inn, and maybe incorporate that story onto our website.

A mysterious phenomenon occurred during this "writing down" process. Even though my fingers were on the keyboard, and I thought that I was in control of my word processor, a novel based on our experiences started to emerge. The story got longer and longer, individuals became composites of different people, and some were made up altogether. Situations were curtailed, exaggerated, or fabricated, until eventually the book took over and I became merely the instrument for words being committed to paper. Not that anything here, even the made up bits, is too outrageous—many innkeepers will identify fully with the situations described here and can probably add to them a thousand times over.

There may be people who, upon reading this account, will think to themselves, "Oh, I know that bed and breakfast," or, "I know who he is talking about," maybe even, "He's talking about me." But you don't know, and I'm not actually quoting or talking about anybody—just using real places and events in the past as guides to help build the story. Dig deeper if you think that you recognize something, and you will come to realize that it may be similar, but then again it is actually different.

One final thought to any aspiring innkeepers who might read this book. Our real inn was purchased just at the end of booming real estate prices and easy financing. The simple math that I described in the story—this much coming in and this much going out, and as long as one is on the plus side over a twelve-month period, no worries—is flawed. In real life, this reasoning leaves a lot to desired, and my fictional character Frank Thornton who said, "You don't need professional help," was wrong. If you *are* thinking of buying a bed and breakfast, you really should consider employing an expert to advise you.

CPSIA information can be obtained at www.ICGtesting.com
Printed in the USA
LVOW080403220413

330214LV00001B/1/P